Flood Stage

An Anthology of Saint Louis
Poets

Matthew Freeman
Anthologist

Best Wishes!
Matthew S. Freeman
7-28-10

Walrus PUBLISHING™

Walrus Publishing, Inc. Saint Louis, MO

First Edition

Title: Robert Lowes
Editor: Lisa Miller
Manuscript Editor: Julie Failla Earhart
Art: Rusti Levin Graphic Design

ISBN 978-0-9844857-3-4

Walrus Publishing, Inc. 4168 Hartford Street, Saint Louis, MO
63116

TABLE OF CONTENTS

FOREWARD

I wrote poetry in isolation for fourteen years, suffering the various breakdowns and beat downs I concluded were necessary to the craft—the ones I've made clear in my own poems and don't need to mention here—and I never really read aloud or got too close to another poet. Yet all along in my head I was thinking that someday I might like to edit a local anthology. Thanks to Lisa Miller and Walrus Publishing that dream has come to pass.

I didn't have much going on in any respect when late in 2004 when I "Googled" "St. Louis Poetry" and found out about the St. Louis Poetry Center, a place to which one can send a draft of a poem to be handled by an experienced critic in the workshop style. Nervous and shy, I arrived having given them no less than three verbose pieces. Soon, I was pleasantly surprised—the eminent poet/painter Ed Boccia took me under his wing straight off, and presently I would become pals with the witty Bob Nazarene. As I was leaving the first workshop, Steven Schreiner, the poet of high stature who had been the critic that month, said, "Matt, keep on writing." Well, those few words kept me going for a couple of weeks.

Soon I would meet so many great poets and patrons—too many to name here—that I literally felt like I'd been given an invitation to the society of the St. Louis in-crowd of poetry. In those early days Dean Grubbs and Nancy Hughes and Loy Ledbetter got me some readings here and there with Ed Boccia, and I'd always try and drag out my friends and family. Suddenly I found out about a lot of different reading series and often enough sweet Karen Mondale would make sure I got to and fro. I recall bugging Aaron Belz and Richard Newman, skilled and popular poets, with my books. They were nice enough to let me read.

After having traveled a bit, stayed in a bit, I was starting to feel at home. I met the beautiful Mary Eden and asked her when she started writing. "Somewhere around twelve." I came back with, "Damn, I must have been a late bloomer...I didn't start till I was seventeen." "Hey," Mary replied, "I didn't have anything to *say* until I was seventeen."

Soon at Duff's, Amy Debrecht and I would share rude jokes and rough drafts; I can't say how much fun it was to make her and Karen Duffy—the city's greatest patron—laugh at some crude witticism...and turn to see jovial Cassandra and Kara and Richard at the end of the bar.

I used to swear I'd never do poetry at an open mike, but I can't say how satisfied I've been by totally abrogating that policy. Julia Gordon-Bramer—another talented angel who's shared coffee and manuscripts and great hospitality—introduced me to the Loudmouth and Wired Coffee open mics: great places to bring works in progress and read them to an eager audience of comrades. It was there that Ken Brown surfaced, a straight- shooter who comes down from Burroughs and the Beats; Lisa Ebert, the sultry poetess/teacher; and of course Amanda Wells, stylish and enthusiastic editor of Literal Chaos.

I remember seeing Joseph Sulier and Mathieu Paul riding their bikes down Arsenal to meet some of us fledgling performers at the Hide-Away, where we talked shop and planned on how we might take over St. Louis with verse. Their series, "Get Born," only recently concluded its hugely popular run at Duff's. Once in a while one of us leaves St. Louis, though...only to come back in the typical fashion. Maybe it's youth and anarchy that make one only more fond of home.

So during these last few years these new friends would habitually give me poems, and I would read them and dole out my meager advice. Every poet in this volume is solid and respected, and I selected the poems for inclusion from a sizable stack. What can anyone say to a poet? Even for the greatly successful it's a hard road—I can hear my father now, almost—and the majority of us labor in anonymity, leaving behind a crazy box of poems to be dealt with when someone's cleaning out the apartment...and that's what this anthology is trying to combat. This book is a record of a very live poetry scene, diverse and of great quality, spread across the whole city. If you wonder about the state of St. Louis poetry, look here: we've got some very skillful practitioners.

When I was wandering around SLU in the early nineties I used to think poetry was a type of magic, a type of dream, a primary process event, as I termed it. And after all the workshops and readings and practical matters I've come full circle; I chose each of these poems because I felt they were the most magical, the ones that had been blessed.

Thanks to all the beautiful poets I've met.

Thanks to my sister, Jessica, without whom there would be no poems.

Thanks to Amanda Wells for all her help in formatting this and providing emotional support, too.

I'd like to also mention two entities of which I was not aware before the completion of this project. First, Exploding Swan, a great group of new young friends at Washington University. Second, JKPublishing, a new house, that's doing great things in this city.

Most of all, thanks to Lisa Miller for taking a chance on us.

Matthew Freeman
Anthologist

Matthew Freeman is the author of The Dogtown Poet *and* Desolation on Delmar, *both available from Ginninderra Press and* Darkness Never Far *is available from Coffeetown Press. He lives in The Loop in St. Louis where he is a full-time poet.*

Sally Van Doren

Sally Van Doren

Sally Van Doren was born and raised in St. Louis. She attended Reed Elementary School and Mary Institute, and then went to boarding school at Phillips Academy in Andover, Massachusetts. She received a B.A. in Comparative Literature from Princeton University. After college, she worked as a writer, radio news director, and arts administrator in Santa Fe and New York City. In 1993, she moved back to St. Louis when her husband, John Van Doren, became the co-owner of Greenberg Van Doren Gallery. After their second child was born, she entered the M.F.A. Program in Creative Writing at the University of Missouri-St. Louis, which she completed in 1999. She has taught Creative Writing for Springboard to Learning/Young Audiences in the St. Louis Public Schools and in the St. Louis County Juvenile Detention Center. She curates the Sunday Workshop Series for the St. Louis Poetry Center.

Van Doren's book, "Sex at Noon Taxes," (LSU Press 2008) won the Walt Whitman Award from the Academy of American Poets. Her poems have appeared in literary magazines such as *American Letters and Commentary, American Poet, Barrow Street, Big Muddy, Boulevard, Colorado Review, Delmar, 5AM, LIT, Margie, The New Republic, Parthenon West Review, Poetry Daily, River Styx, Southwest Review, 2River and Verse Daily.* Her poem, "Preposition," is featured as an animated film in the Poetry Foundation's Poetry Everywhere program.

She enjoys giving poetry readings and has been invited to give readings at universities, community colleges, high schools, elementary schools, bookstores, libraries, book festivals, correction facilities, bars and art museums in Missouri, Connecticut, New York, and New Jersey. She writes most mornings after her children have gone to school. She is working on a new manuscript of poems and also revising and editing another. She writes one line every day in "The Sense Series," a 1400-line long poem that she calls a "contemporaneous epic."

Van Doren finds inspiration for her work from a wide range of sources such as poetry and poetic theory she is reading or has read, classes she has taught, places she has been, emotional and physical situations she has been in, art and artists she has encountered, her children's homework assignments, word games, music, food, the weather, and current events.

I Teach After Anger Management

The morning starts ajar, jarred as it were,
by the jolt of sunrise, the end of nocturnal
evasion, and it is jarring. Get in the car,
drive to work. Take North Grand to the
old Water Tower. Lock the doors.
Switch into a mode which allows you
to speak and act with authority, despite
the coldness tightening the middle vertebrae
of your neck. By hour two, you notice
a loosening, you perform, shake hands,
say, "I'm glad to be here." Lunch in the car,
whole wheat bread with bits of nuts. Let
your eyes close once or twice. Open them.
There is one house across from the school
with all its windows intact, blue curtains
on the left, white on the right. A teenager in a
sweatshirt that hangs to his knees
knocks and enters. A fire truck whips by
on West Florissant. Ring the buzzer, wait
for the click and climb the stairs to the last class.
The 26 fourth graders are up for, up for,
what are they up for? Out of their desks,
on the floor, all after the one pink marker
to decorate their new folders. Precious,
LaShaye, Destiny, Anshaniqua. There is
a freeway which connects to an interstate
to take you home. Drive it, avoiding the
construction
median on the left, the veering truck on the right.
Park in the driveway and don't get out. Roll
down the window. Acknowledge the January thaw.
Look into the early afternoon sun. Morning is long
gone.
Morning is irretrievable.

My Alphabet

I like to flirt with words,
to whore myself out
to a vernacular, to suck
up to syntax, to be
the girl in the room
whose shirt is see-
through, whose lips
lure the gentlemen
from their genres.
I tutor my suitors
in the art of the tease,
but if someone tries
to buy me, they'll
find I'm overpriced.
I won't settle for
less than everything.

CAR ACCIDENTS
WHIPLASH
INJURED
CHILDREN
CLOSED
FUTURE FORCLOSURE
FORCLOSURE

Lorin Cuoco

Lorin Cuoco

Lorin Cuoco grew up in Lebanon, Illinois. She received her Bachelor's degree from Southern Illinois University at Edwardsville and her Master of Arts in Liberal Arts from St. John's College in Santa Fe, New Mexico. A former public radio reporter, based in St. Louis, Cuoco filed stories on the arts for *Morning Edition, All Things Considered,* and *Performance Today*, and produced broadcasts for NPR World of Opera. She also produced a weekly poetry program, *Ars Poetica*, a series of literary profiles and the radio play *The Coffee Room* by Stanley Elkin.

With writer William Gass, Cuoco established the International Writers Center at Washington University in 1990 and served as its associate director until 2001. She is the editor of six books including *The Writer in Politics, The Writer and Religion, The Dual Muse: the Writer As Artist, the Artist As Writer* and *Literary St. Louis: A Guide*. Her poetry, interviews and other writings have appeared in *New Letters, The Review of Contemporary Fiction, River Styx, Sou'Wester* and *St. Louis Magazine*. She was a Lannan Writer in Residence in Marfa, Texas, in 2002.

Cuoco served as producer of *The Tunnel Audiobook,* as read by William Gass, published by Dalkey Archive Press in 2006. She lives in University City.

Love among the Loonies

My thoughts are with you tonight, Alcibiades
we saw the best minds in a generation
walking the hall looking for a nursely fix
your room, aseptically cleaned,
has seen many since you
but none so brave nor none so knowing
none able to admit insanity.

There was your breeze just now
your ghost stalking the hall
remembrance of the one night
they unshackled you—
you wanted Revelations
and I gave you Ezra Pound.

There once again your shadow, breeze
ghost in benign haunt
I think that you have thought
it there only to taunt me
as I sit here hallucinating, listening
to the snores of the manics and the panics
to alcoholics and the whores.

Engagement

After calling each other dear in the pleasantest sort of way—
Menelaus and Helen in a wink, Vladimir and Vera,
Penelope and Odysseus—we need but insert
the dream where only its glimpse resided and scrutinize
the pleasures Shaw felt so guilty of. Poor Shaw, G. B.

No, it has not much to do with love, as all the men say, but
it is more fun. And is there more? And will the essays come?
The post mortems? And is the sadness greater? This marriage
to convenience wins converts and men's rue, does not erase scars

nor exalt romance or bring beauteous words. It's not that we
didn't have a good beginning, but we don't have to go back.
Can't. Won't. No wedding poems writ by unbelieving hand:
the hand operates on faith.

Julia Gordon-Bramer

Julia Gordon-Bramer

Having grown up outside of Washington D.C., Julia Gordon-Bramer came to St. Louis by force in 1989, when her then-husband had a job opportunity and family there. They split, and she and her two children got the opportunity to recreate their lives. Since then, she's had a lot of adventures: working with famous writers; starting a rock magazine; and marrying her favorite lead-guitarist.

As director of the Writers Voice literary center, Gordon-Bramer's worked with luminaries in literature such as Ken Kesey, Allen Ginsberg, and Gloria Steinem, to name just a few. Her poetry and fiction awards include: Carve Magazine's 2007 Raymond Carver Short Story Contest, the St. Louis Writers Guild's Deane Wagner Poetry Contest, the Margaret Leong Poetry award, finalist for the national William Faulkner Pirate's Alley Novel-in-Progress Creative Writing Award, and she was recently nominated for the national Best New Poets. She is a board member of River Styx literary magazine, a Member of the St. Louis Poetry Center, and a multiple-year Member of Distinction with the St. Louis Writers Guild.

Gordon-Bramer is also author of a memoir, *NIGHT TIMES*, currently seeking publication, and she has a non-fiction book in the works on Sylvia Plath and a collection of her poetry is expected out in 2012. Julia's award-winning poetry and prose has or will soon appear in *Plath Profiles*, *The Arkansas Review: Journal of Delta Studies*, *MARGIE: The American Journal of Poetry*, Cornell University's *Rainy Day*, *Carve* magazine, *Santa Fe Writers Project*, *Clemson Poetry Review*, and many more. She holds an M.F.A. in Creative Writing for both poetry and fiction from the University of Missouri-St. Louis. She teaches English at St. Louis Community College, which forced her to finally understand the proper use of the comma.

University of Missouri – St. Louis Library, During a Storm

Thunder shakes the fifth floor where I sit
closest to the roof, to feel it better
To watch light flicker, lick
at both wet and dry sides of window glass
Tamed and untamed the electric
empty level, this one I
like best with the research no one reads
at these tables clean of debris
except for me and a shiny penny;
we are kin as clutter here and not
worth much without a lot of help
Low mumbling distant rumbling voices from
somewhere
far from this forest of tall shelves, microfiche, binders
The signs say No
Noise but who are we kidding?
If a tree falls, and all that… I fight
the urge to scream, just
to do it, because I could, because I won't
be caught. Outside the mirror violence of my brain
subsides to gentle rain and alone here how
in peace, I think:
I preferred the storm.

Punks

They called us “Punks” as we dropped our trash: icy
wax paper soda cups and Big Mac packs in steel blue
mail box slots, skipped class and called The Office
from the cafeteria payphone, threatening bombs
during exams. We ran through gardens and picked
rose bushes bare, owning the wilting blooms in our
tangled hair, walked empty lots at night and shrieked
at the top of our lungs, then played dumb watching
the brave run to help, as the afraid called the cops.
We shoplifted candy and cigarettes, crank-called
Help lines, stood pretty at the gas station, bumming
change three days straight, for beer on the weekend.
We thumbed into the city to taunt Johns leaving
porno shops. Borrowed each other’s everythings
without asking, scammed all kinds of drugs and slept
with bed-spinning boys to trick their hearts. We
sneered at our supposed blessings, at all the bullshit
promises made to us, like: Barbie doll bodies,
          back-to-school-shopping,
allowance,   prom dresses, dates at the drive-in,
               college education,
                    Sunday family dinners,
                         help with homework,
a ride to a friend’s house,

               an interested ear.

Therapy

Let's discuss that
inappropriate
commentjudgmentactionlaughter

(I speak and decide for myself.
How can you
know what's best?
I don't accept it.
It was meant to be
funny! Isn't it
funny?)

Why do you fight? Talk some
more about
mommydaddydrugsdrinkrapehatelovealone
How you are feeling right
now. Why
do you push back
cuticles, feelings, fidget, change
the way you sit, it's more
than learning to trust
the gut

(I never could)

[scribble scribble]

That's because you've been trained
not to trust your brain, eyes, ears, skin
where boundaries end and where
you begin if you want to
get better, do you want to?

(I don't know.
This is honest. I'm just

afraid to be anything
less than me
because me has never been
enough)

It's not just
honest or lies, it's not just
total love or
trust no one, no it's not just
young or dead, it's not just
black or white, here
have a Kleenex…

(but I've blown
out the grays and I don't wanna live
removed from dark deep,
I don't wanna live
in that shallow middle
mediocre eating burgers
and Prozac with a six-pack
watching grayscale sitcoms.
I don't wanna stop
at classic rock, grow slow and soft
sometimes I
don't wanna live
when resolution's cost
is authenticity
feeling so far
nothing's made it
go away, so…
Go away.
You won.
You made me
cry).

You've come a long way.
Don't forget your co-pay.
See you next week.

Amy S. Debrecht

Amy S. Debrecht

Amy S. Debrecht received her M.F.A. in poetry writing from the University of Missouri-St. Louis, where she was actively involved with the literary journal *Natural Bridge*. She is an Associate Editor for a medical publisher in St. Louis and an active volunteer ftor the literary journal *River Styx*. She also writes book reviews for *Pleiades* magazine. Her poems have appeared in *Natural Bridge*, *Sou'wester*, *Poet Lore*, and *Flint Hills Review*.

Past the candle's last falter snow floats

From a pink sky leaves a cap on the lamppost
The dog's snout tunnels through short drifts
Our prints softly covered the next lap around
Every moment we walk through our own vanishing
No bells in the morning no blackbirds on the sill
The kettle calls like a ship from the kitchen
Great columns of ice collapse inside downspouts
If there is nothing new in the world
Enter headlong the flame of pristine fields
Trespass through beauty you shouldn't know
You must concede that something is left
That lasts worthy of our glances
That time is not a turncoat

Zero Rue de Nowhere

You live on a mountain peak.
You live on an ocean floor.
You live in a castle's keep
    surrounded by a moat.
You live in an unmoored boat.
You live in a cave guarded by a bear.
You live at Zero Rue de Nowhere.
You live in a mansion and the butler won't be bribed.
You live in a queen bee's hive.
You live in a hurricane's eye.
You live in the belly of a whale.
You live in an igloo at the farthest, farthest pole.
You live in your own brambled soul
    that will not set you free,
    and where does that leave me?
With no rope, no air,
no bridge, no oar,
no lure, no map,
no coin, no swarm,
no cellar, no light,
no sled, no scythe.

Cassandra Howard

Cassandra Howard

Cassandra Howard likes the words "mister," "buster," and "jerk." Her poetry has appeared in *Quarterly West.*

Letter to My Ex, Who I Left Without Explaining

Dear Illinois,

You two were close, I know. But, I was impressed.
He told me his name was misi-ziibi, Great River,
gichi-ziibi, Big River, Father of Waters, messip.
Flood plains, confluences, sandbars, all things
riverine were on my mind when I was with you.

I hopped in somewhere near Alton, dizzy
with wanderlust, thought he'd show me around,
who knows how far south. He raged for me now,
despite his history running from state to state.
I'm embarrassed to admit how long it took me
to notice the others – martini-ed vacationers
aboard a yacht, thirty orange-vested tourists on deck
some outdated steamboat, floaters trailing six-packs,
fishers casting from banks and jon boats.
He had bikini-clad bathers in every tributary.

Now and then, I cross bridges, never looking down,
to walk your flat plains and scratchy cornfields
pungent as sexed bodies. Clandestine owls hoot,
then swoop, wing air in my eardrums. Still I hear
water splashing the bluffs, rushing above stones,
spilling, lapping, tinkling over the shallows.
Voice of the river, an eddy on dry land, turns me
on my heels back across that bridge.

If I return to you the way I left, would you
take me back? If I dolphin wiggle, backstroke,
breaststroke,
freestyle, doggy paddle, butterfly, mermaid, floating
corpse,
one-after-the-other-arm my way back to you?

Missouri substitutes well enough. He's taller,
more social, but like you.

Keith Byler

Keith Byler

Keith Byler is a native St. Louisian now living across the river out in the boondocks of southern Illinois, somewhere north of Edwardsville. Byler is a physician who spent ten years in the trenches of the emergency room and is now in private practice. His poems have appeared *in Emergency: True Stories From the Nation's E.R.'s, Hurricane Blues, MARGIE: The American Journal of Poetry, Untamed Ink,* as well as his medical school newspaper *Still Kickin'*. He is also a winner of the Metro Arts in Transit 2008 Poetry in Motion Contest. Byler is active in the St. Louis Poetry Center and currently serves as its board president.

Peace on Earth

I could tell you that it was a crisp, clear winter night
outside the E.R.
of St. Elsewhere Regional Hospital,

with incandescent stars burning holes
through the coal-black tapestry above,
Orion's belt blazing,
the Seven Sisters suspended like a small bright kite,
and a moon's silver silver in rotating skies
taking flight
over the rooftop of the south tower.

Or I could I say that the sky was an overcast
battleship gray
with the clean bracing scent of winter
(you know that smell),
and snowflakes the size of golf balls
floating down from the heavens
alighting on my eyelashes and tongue
turning the world into a snow-globe scene
from Currier & Ives.

But it was just another frigid sooty night
when I escaped to the ambulance bay

shivering in my scrubs
and Birkenstock clogs
gripping my thin white lab coat
against the bluster,
stethoscope chilling around my neck,

ducking out for a rare forbidden smoke
and a quiet moment of Christmas Eve

Peace on Earth Goodwill to Men

with smokestacks
from the refinery across the way
belching fire and brimstone

and an ambulance in the bay
expelling diesel fumes.
"It needs a tune-up,"
I told the paramedic as he
changed the sheets on the gurney.

And a siren in the distance
("God, I hope it's not coming here...")
as I scanned the cityscape horizon
across the ink-black ribbon of river

no Santa in sight

while just inside the hissing pneumatic doors
the battlefield of horrors
waited:

sick babies
and kids with earaches and snotty noses,
an old man with chest pain
possibly getting ready to

Sleep In Heavenly Peace

a sixteen year old having a miscarriage,
an ankle fracture from a slip on the ice,
and a frequent-flyer psych patient
with an overdose.

I tossed the cigarette after three quick puffs,
feeling guilty for taking the two seconds
heading back inside to do what I could
although on this night in particular

it felt so like trying to empty
the ocean with a teacup.

I noticed that daylight was peeking purple over the
top of the city,

Jupiter chasing waning crescent moon across the
soon-quickening sky.

Presently long shadows would drop dead from the
sides of skyscrapers

like prostrate, ready for their circular sundial labors
timing the sessions of the Christmas day aborning.

The day was waking up, and I thought that Mrs.
Claus

must have been busy late into the night at my house
Santa being otherwise indisposed in hell

for the past twenty-two hours
wanting only to finish his shift and beat feet for home

Over the river and through the woods

home to a house hopefully still dark
with slumber, kids snuggled in,
and my wife restless-sleepless
in a bed too large for one
especially on Christmas morn.

Compression

Sitting by your bed
watching your chest rise and
fall with each soft hiss,
holding your insensate hand
still warm and pink

On the floor
in the corner
behind the I.V. pole
resides a crescent of dust
the shape of a quarter moon
left day by day
by the arc of the housekeeper's
dry-mop,

Dust composed
of so many dried tiny shards
of skin, detritus of hair,
sweet-smelling baby powder
slopped over the mattress edge,
coughs dehydrated in mid-air,
flakes of tears,
and all other manner of cosmic stuff,

Dust as we all become,
although you sooner than later,
you with the sardonic humors
who joked that you were
ready for your baptism
of fire.

And me preparing for that awkward moment
a few days hence, a knock on the door,

when I receive your ample 6'2" frame
compressed tightly into a cardboard container
the size of the soft-sided lunch box
you used to carry to work each day.

Cassandra Bannon

Cassandra Bannon

Cassandra Bannon's military brat mother wanted a safe place to root her family and chose St. Louis—in part because of its strong arts community with a world-renowned museum, zoo, and symphony. While the pristine backdrop of Ladue was safe, the personality of the culture and its inherent social inequities did not often mirror the environment.

Those inequities often vexed young Bannon, but encouraged by the arts community—like her Mom before her—she writes, works, and plays in an attempt to foster positive change. Whether working in healthcare quality, performing in local theatre, writing with a feminist poetry collective, volunteering to advocate for foster children in the city, or applying to law school, she is proud to call St. Louis home.

Red

Nancy Reagan ruined the color for me
during my formative years when excess
reigned and nobody minded. Before we lost sad boys
out west, when columbine was just a flower.
Our towers still loomed high –
we felt mighty and the world
seemed to believe us. I didn't realize
how much I liked that color.

A hazy recollection of happy times –
bows all over, especially in hair and crisp
white table linens that live in the freezer until ironed.

Red was a color of celebration, high holidays
filled with sweets and trinkets spilling out of socks
or shoe boxes well adorned.
Rain boots that fit over your shoes
all the best pie fillings, hard candy too.
In the summer it was the
color of citizen's pride, power and courage.

She wore it and her bobble head gazed adoringly
at a man who made lying seem patriotic. He called
her
Mommy, a poster child to the dressing class –

Power elite. The world was awash with men in
crimson battle ties with sharp ladies all following
suit.
Scarves and pill box hats like Jackie-O but not.
Shirts coordinated with pumps or bags of a similar
hue.
All a unified message to us. I turned to black.

Did she bring that with her?

John J. Han

John J. Han

John J. Han has been living in St. Louis County since 1999. A native of South Korea, he came to the United States in 1988, earning his M.A. in English from Kansas State University and his Ph.D. in English from the University of Nebraska-Lincoln. He also holds a B.A. in English language and literature and an M.Ed. in English teaching from Korea, as well as a Writing Certificate in English from Missouri Baptist University in St. Louis.

Han is currently a Professor of English and chair of the Humanities Division at Missouri Baptist University where he teaches courses in literature and creative writing. Han is also an active member of the St. Louis Poetry Center and St. Louis Writers Guild. His *haiku* and *senryu* have appeared in various venues including the *Mainichi Daily News* (Tokyo, Japan), *Cantos: A Literary and Arts Magazine*, *Collegian*, and *In Other Words*; his "In the Yard: Senryu" won an Honorable Mention in the 2008 James H. Nash Poetry Contest.

He has conducted workshops on Japanese poetic types at E. H. Lyle Academy in downtown St. Louis, at Borders in Ballwin, and at Morgan County High School. He is completing the manuscript for his first poetry book, tentatively entitled *Little Guy Haiku: Bailey, a Maltese.* He has also translated dozens of Mr. Song Su-kwon's lyric poems from Korean into English which he seeks to publish as a book.

Being an Asian-American: Senryu

1
Upon no request
The waitress brings me chopsticks
We both smile

2
The Chinese waiter
Keeps saying, "Thank you, sir,"
Until I blush

3
On the street—
Barry doesn't remember
I am his neighbor

4
She is Asian, yet
Her hair is as yellow as
Forsythia

5
A TV ad
Is an Asian there?
Yes, in the corner

6
Clark says, "Watch out, Jim!
John knows karate."
I ask, "What's karate?"

Fragments from Japan: Haiku

1
Her brief, fragrant smile
Turns into a butterfly
That keeps fluttering

2
Amida Buddha
The eyes half-closed, downcast
Above the din

3
Apart from the crowd
Eyes fixed on the Buddha
She clasps her lily hands

4
Shrine at sunrise
Wearing shoes wet with dew
She invokes the gods

5
Pouring rain
I watch TV all day long
In the hotel room

Philip Gounis

Philip Gounis

Philip John Gounis (born February 1, 1948, Richmond Heights, Missouri) is an American poet, literary journalist, archivist, filmmaker, publisher, concert, and book reviewer.

Gounis first came into public awareness in the early 1970s when he and several colleagues filmed and presented a series of experimental films. These films were the product of the informal largess of the University of Missouri-St. Louis. During this period Gounis also began to publish his poetry in several alternative press outlets and read on KDNA FM radio. Some of the participants in these readings later formed the nucleus of *River Styx* literary magazine.

In March 1976, he initiated a weekly blues program on KCLC radio at Lindenwood College in St. Charles, Missouri. *Crackerbox* featured recorded blues music spanning five decades and sometimes hosted guests such as Grammy winner Corky Siegel, Linda LaFlamme (*It's a Beautiful Day*), boogie- woogie virtuoso Rudy "Silver Cloud" Coleman, blues master Bob Case, and others. In June 1976 he began to host and produce *Verbatim*, a monthly showcase of poetry and music. Poets Donald Finkel, Jan Garden Castro, Carter Revard, and Michael Castro were some of the poets featured.

In the early 1980s Gounis contributed to the work of the Soulard Culture Squad. This group of poets and musicians performed throughout the historic Soulard area and published several poetry collections.

In 1988, he co-founded a magazine of politics and popular culture, *Steamshovel Press* with the impetus of publishing an interview with Ram Dass. At the end of the decade and into the '90s he took part in radio programs such as *Off The Beaten Path, Poetry Beat* and *Literature for the Halibut* on KDHX FM in St. Louis, Missouri. Some of the transcripts of his interviews done in conjunction with these programs are available at the Washington University Department of Special Collections Olin Library. In summer 2005, Intangible Studios released the compact disk, *Form Matters* on which Gounis collaborated with musician Rich Kruse. *Some Of These Have Appeared*, a chapbook of poetry was published spring 2007.

Fraud

we first met back in the retail record racks
squeezed together by the Hot Sax
it was surreptitious
she was tricky
she undressed
Prince
with her eyes
and it was only conversation
that was there
in the way

she liked my boots
she loved my boots
she adored my boots
she adored snakeskin

she moved in with my parents
she kicked me out
losing the Sun
I lived for adventure only

driving a clunking fork lift truck
up and down drab aisles
of dank, endless, dark, industrial warehouse
mazes
so adventurous

later

tuned to the black
radio station far out
in the night
kneeling on the cobblestones
pleading
in the snow

summer trousers ripped
chipped buttons
on my short sleeved shirt
long time broken and lost
feverish

now

praying for the sky
to light up
to find my way

Impasse

she played a gleaming cello
on the mountain top
when Minnesota was a tropical resort
now she's on the skids

mama, why can't you hear us anymore

is it true
that you use
the same ear plugs
that Marie Antoinette did?

Breaths

reading about
projective verse by
Charles Olson
but thinking about you

my mind drifting
to you and your final
puffs of breath

eyes closed
your strength rapidly dissipating
as you lie in your bed of transformation

years before
when the children were much younger
I had tried to explain to them about the mystery
simply, naively
as if I knew…

"When someone dies, it's like the air going out
of a balloon," I demonstrated.
"Sometimes it's suddenly, sometimes it's gradually,
but then the balloon lies limp and still. The air
goes out everywhere. You can't see it, but you can
feel it. That's what Spirit is like."

and as I remember this
and as I write this
a lilting breeze enters
thru my open window
and scatters
all of my papers and poems
and my feathery
weightless conceits

Richard Newman

Richard Newman

Richard Newman has lived in St. Louis for nearly twenty-five years. He has worked a variety of stupid jobs in this town: housepainter, maintenance worker and groundskeeper at Tower Grover Park, community organizer, copyeditor for a corporate computer magazine, composition instructor, housepainter again, singer/songwriter/guitarist in several rock-n-roll bands, freelance writer, and clerk at St. Louis Public Library's Central Branch. One of the few jobs he applied for and actually landed was the worst job in his whole life: a copymonkey at Kinko's in Clayton.

Newman currently teaches poetry and creative writing at St. Louis Community College at Florissant Valley and Washington University and in UMSL's Honor's College. For the last 15 years he has served as editor of *River Styx* magazine, and he also co-directs the River Styx at Duff's Reading Series.

He is the author of the poetry collection *Borrowed Towns* (Word Press, 2005) and the forthcoming collection *Domestic Fugues* (Steel Toe Boots, 2009), as well as several chapbooks, including *24 Tall Boys: Dark Verse for Light Times* (Snark Publishing/Firecracker Press, 2007), *Monster Gallery:19 Terrifying and Amazing Monster Sonnets!* (Snark Publishing, 2005), *Tastes Like Chicken and Other Meditations* (Snark Publishing, 2004), and *Greatest Hits* (Pudding House, 2002). His poems have appeared in *Best American Poetry 2006, Boulevard, Crab Orchard Review, New Letters* (subsequent winner of the 2007 Reader's Choice Award), *Poetry Daily, Southern Poetry Review, The Sun, Tar River Poetry, 32 Poems, Verse Daily*, and many other periodicals and anthologies. Newman was recently named "Best Local Poet" in the 2008 *Riverfront Times* "Best of St. Louis" edition, which sandwiched him somewhere between "Best Hair on a TV Personality" and "Best Strip Club."

He lives in Benton Park with his daughter, Natalie, whose poem appeared on busses and Metrolink as part of the Metro Arts in Transit Project, and his wife, Kara, who also has a poem in this anthology. Their evenings usually entail somber poetry readings and earnest literary discussions, as well as hatching plans to make millions when the three of them take over the poetry world.

Delay

He sat on the porch, sipped his can of Stroh's.
Dinner's ready! He delayed coming inside.
Instead he looked over the rows and rows
of houses, contemplated stars that died
eons ago but only now reached him.
After the third call, he grabbed another
beer and moved into the dining room,
sat down among his children and their mother.
That night, when the kids slept, tempers would flair.
For now they had sloppy joes and Tater Tots.
They had leftovers in tight-lipped Tupperware,
and so they chose to savor his small draught
of calm, so cool and bland but also stable,
and flash dead smiles across the dinner table.

Please Be Advised

You are being watched for your protection –
and we protect you everywhere, recorded
for your convenience. Please wait for inspection.

We even track your chewing gum selection
so all your purchases can be rewarded.
You are being taped. For your protection

we monitor each internet erection.
We know your deepest wants, however sordid.
For your convenience, please spread for inspection.

Wait, hurry. You must not miss your connection.
There is no jumping off this plane once boarded.
You are being locked in for your protection.

Your shadow in shade will not escape detection.
Be grateful for the kindness we've afforded.
For your convenience, please permit inspection.

We have even captured your reflection.
Pay no attention how this form is worded.
Sign on the broken line for your protection,
for your convenience, and prepare for inspection.

Hate Mail

They often come on little thank you cards,
cowardly dribs and drabs, pastiches of hate.
The handwriting and word choice always feel
familiar. Never signed. I don't even
know anybody else who receives hate mail,
licked and sealed with the stubbornest spit.

Some are exes, some e-mailed, one scary:
we know where you live, we see you every day,
we have big plans for you. This January,
after an extremely loving year,
I opened two hate letters in one day.
I confess it made me feel important.

One curlicued, *You were a terrible teacher*
and an even worse human being.
My plans were ruined, my money stolen,
and my life has never been the same –
are you still so very pleased with your self?
from one whose name is writ in water.

The other said it with a rubber stamp:
FORM-LETTER REJECTS ARE SO CRASS
JUST SHOVE THIS ONE RIGHT UP YOUR ASS
AND THEN DROP DEAD, GO TO HELL TOO
AND TAKE YOUR DAMN LETTER WITH YOU!
It's pretty clear why we rejected him.

If only they'd include their name and address,
I'd mail back every single hate note, adding,
I hate you back! Love, Richard. Fuck you, I tried
my best. Love, Richard. I'm sorry. Love, Richard.

Forgive me, please! Love Richard, Please Love Richard!
hate barely showing through the other side.

Eamonn Wall

Eamonn Wall

A native of Ireland who has lived in the USA since 1982, Eamonn Wall arrived in St. Louis in 2000 to take up a position as Smurfit-Stone Professor of Irish Studies at the University of Missouri-St. Louis. At UMSL, Wall teaches courses in Irish Studies and Creative Writing and is director of UMSL's Irish Summer School, held each year in Galway, a sister city of St. Louis'.

Wall enjoys St. Louis for many reasons, most notably because it is such a literary city with a long history of accommodating, encouraging, and producing writers. Also, it is a city rich in its Irish connections, with Irish emigrants settling here in advance of the Louisiana Purchase and making important imprints on the city and its surrounding areas.

His first poems were published in his teens, during college in community magazines in Ireland. As a child, he was encouraged to develop his interests in reading and writing. In his late teens, he decided that he wanted to become a teacher and a writer and, except for odd jobs here and there as a housepainter, bartender, ice-cream factory operative, and door-to-door salesman (from which he was fired after one day), he has followed no other profession.

To date, Wall has published five collections of poetry with Salmon Publishing in Ireland. His most recent collection is *A Tour of Your Country* (2008). His poetry has appeared in various anthologies including *The Book of Irish American Poetry* (University of Notre Dame Press, 2007). *From the Sin-e Café to the Black Hills: Notes on the New Irish* (University of Wisconsin Press, 2000) received the Durkan Prize from the American Conference for Irish Studies for excellence in scholarship. His website is www.eamonnwall.net. He lives in Webster Groves.

Evening on a Back Road

Scattered sheets of cloud and a late burst of sunlight
tangle with tree limb and oak leaf between the seaside

and Camolin. I drive blinded again on the back road
by an old sun falling away to the Blackstairs' mast.

For all these years along this route, I have called out
to a fat church spire at the end of a line of yew trees

that never could despoil the ripened shamelessness
of fields bedded on layers of wet marl. Beasts heave

and breathe, the road bends over the humped bridge.
This road is within me, so blindly drifting: it is itself

& the wind's lone gray substitute, as full of movement
as the railway's sleepers are dipped in creosote and

fixed to a narrow gauge. Cows swing from the church
bell's rope. Sugar beets bolt from the ground. As the

strawberry absorbs the dew, the widower discounts
the news. The priest's housekeeper has turned-up his

stereo to twenty-five. Meeting the River Bann at the
main road, I pick from neon each yellow of the village:

A petrol station, Wexford flags, and the Parkside Bar.
So then! The road straightens. The car picks up speed.

Mother and Daughter Aubade

The architect had curved the great roof and blue
neon of the new arena toward the Missouri River.

At dawn when I awake & pull the blinds, I see a plane
having crossed the river soar over trees high on the Iowa side.

Breezy western light & weird voices cackle nightly
with the talk at my mother's table though, then or now,

like snow geese, the old ground has pulled us back into another time.
There's static: peeled oranges and lemons of daylight &

the sound of the sea at the end of July – on a white evening
bench outside the kitchen door, Old Tom Roberts reads his paper;

pigeons peck at this slippers on an autumn morning; snow falls
on the tall coat stand & front walkway of his block.

Around this kitchen table, folded-in like winter rhododendrons,
my lovely women are gamely sleeping on, light not yet

having flooded with the river our hotel room & I would bet that
the bricks of the streets are as cool & as smooth as their soft faces.

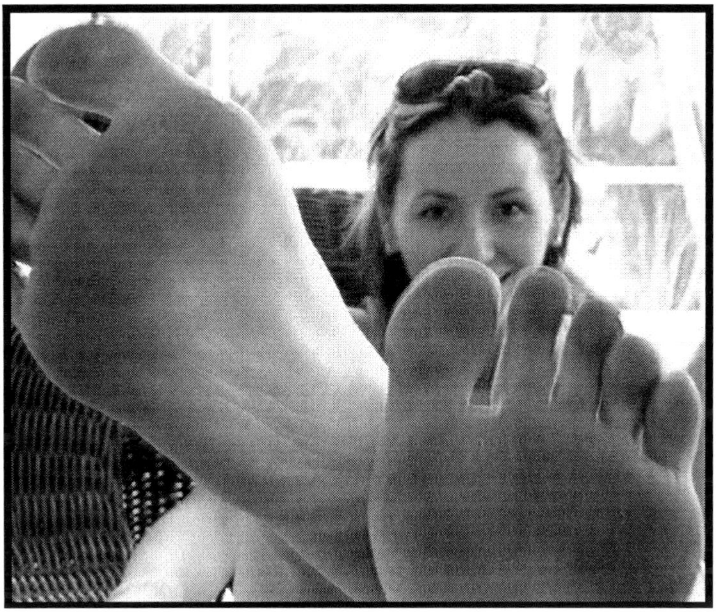

Kara Moyer

Kara Moyer

Kara Moyer was born and raised in St. Louis, more specifically the suburbs of North County. Answering the age-old St. Louis-based question, she graduated high school from Hazelwood Central and earned a B.A. in English with an emphasis in Creative Writing from Webster University. For the last six years she has lived in various parts of St. Louis city, therefore discovering the best Indian buffets and sushi restaurants and enjoying living in the middle of the Midwest more than she ever thought she could—despite the weather in February. She currently lives in the Historic Benton Park neighborhood, teaches poetry through Springboard, and sells divine home furnishings at Pier 1 Imports.

Although she grew up as a spoiled only child and was told repeatedly that she could be anything she wanted, Kara ignored all practical avenues and became a poet. Writing has since become an integral part of her life as much as navigating around St. Louis road construction. She thinks poetry is the most rewarding form of writing as long as it's poignant, fresh, and imaginative. Formal poetry has always held a special place in her heart, particularly the works of Robert Frost and Edna St. Vincent Millay.

In 2004, Kara won 1st place in the League for Innovation's National Poetry Contest. She spent her award money on a new bicycle, a fancy pair of black boots, and many fine buckets of beer at her favorite pub-in-the-wall, Cat's Meow, in Soulard. She also had a recipe for the best Cajun shrimp and pineapple skewers published in *New Southerner*, an online literary magazine. Her poems have appeared in *32 Poems*, *Natural Bridge*, and *PMS: poemmemoirstory*.

Future plans involve earning an M.F.A. in poetry from a low-residency program. She also plans to transform her cocktail napkin-sized backyard into a prosperous vegetable garden, resurrect her interest in photography, run a 5 ½ -minute mile, visit various beaches around the world that have yet to be populated with tourists, join a co-ed basketball league that she and her husband, poet Richard Newman, can dominate, and produce a damn fine book of poems.

Elegy for a Love

Forget about the Calico
who pitter-patters near the door.
She doesn't purr to lick our wounds.

And never mind the rising yeast,
decanting Cabernet, despite
an idle hand, a wary gaze.

What lingers now – the over-ripe
tomatoes, steeping chamomile,
a brown banana curling in
to hide its bruises – will linger on.

Their patience long outlasts our own,
collecting dust our skins have shed
in quiet doses of the days.

So let's be still inside the sheets,
our knees aligned, at rest (for now),
like silverware inside its drawer.

We've all seen petals scatter floors
though water soaks their deepest roots.

Howard Schwartz

Howard Schwartz

Howard Schwartz is Professor of English at the University of Missouri-St. Louis. He has published three books of poetry, *Vessels*, *Gathering the Sparks*, and *Sleepwalking Beneath the Stars*, and several books of fiction, *including The Four Who Entered Paradise* and *Adam's Soul*. He has also edited a four-volume set of Jewish folktales, which includes *Elijah's Violin & Other Jewish Fairy Tales*, *Miriam's Tambourine: Jewish Folktales from Around the World*, *Lilith's Cave: Jewish Tales of the Supernatural* and, most recently, *Gabriel's Palace: Jewish Mystical Tales*. Schwartz has also edited three major anthologies.

Reimagining the Bible: The Storytelling of the Rabbis, was a finalist for the National Jewish Book Award for 1999. In addition, Schwartz has also published ten children's books, including *The Diamond Tree*, which won the Sydney Taylor Book Award in 1992, *Next Year in Jerusalem: 3000 Years of Jewish Tales*,which won the National Jewish Book Award and the Aesop Award of the American Folklore Society, both in 1996, A *Coat for the Moon* with Barbara Rush, which won Anne Izard Storyteller's Choice Award for 1998 and the 1999 Honor Title of the Storytelling World Awards, and *The Day the Rabbi Disappeared: Jewish Holiday Tales of Magic*, which won the National Jewish Book Award and The Aesop Prize of the American Folklore Society for 2000. His book *Tree of Souls: The Mythology of Judaism*, won the National Jewish Book Award in 2005, and his children's book *Before You Were Born* won the Koret Jewish Book Award the same year. His most recent book is *Leaves from the Garden of Eden: One Hundred Classic Jewish Tales.*

Schwartz lives in St. Louis with his wife Tsila, a calligrapher. He has his three children, Shira, Nati, and Miriam.

Sleepwalking Beneath the Stars

She seems to float
no higher than a hand's breadth
across the field.
Somehow
she knows exactly where she is going,
as if her eyes were open,
as if a falling star had imprinted itself
on her palm,
as if her palm were a map of the orchard
she has entered,
a Braille landscape
waiting to be
read.

By now you know
how dangerous it would be
to wake her—
the star
that rises and sets in her hand
would begin to fade,
the names of the leaves would be lost.
Still
even the slightest wind
threatens to carry her off,
her frail image almost lost in the darkness
as she passes between
the trees.

Even now
the stars hide their light
and every blossom holds its breath.
If the plague of darkness lasts much longer,
she too may be enslaved by silence
and never emerge from the orchard
in peace.

Signs of the Lost Tribe

One day
I found the first sign:
old boxes stacked in the attic
in a room I had never entered.
After that
I found the signs everywhere:
in every drawer I opened,
on every doorpost I passed,
when I lay down
and when I rose up.

Somehow
one of the ten lost tribes
had wandered
out of the desert,
and all of them were living
in my house.

Since then
I have become accustomed
to their ways.
Of course
I never acknowledge
their presence.
Who knows
what they would do
if their secret were known?

They have traveled in exile
ever since they were born,
following the path of the exodus
wherever it leads them.
Somehow
they still fulfill
the rituals
carved out
of so many years of wandering:

blessing the moon,
counting the stars,
casting their sins into the water.

During the day
they search everywhere
for the land that has been lost.
At night
they hide
from the unsuspecting
in closets filled with invisible families,
in drawers crowded with sorrows,
on shelves full of their sad
songs.

They even inhabit
my dreams.
There
above all
they are at home.

Ed Boccia

Ed Boccia

Edward Boccia was born in Newark, New Jersey in 1921. He has been an artist all his life, with paintings and drawings in numerous collections in the United States, Europe and South America. After he received his B.S. and M.A. degrees from Columbia University in New York, he came to St. Louis where he taught painting and drawing in the School of Fine Arts, at Washington University.

Boccia appreciates St. Louis; it's not one of the huge and overcrowded cities, and therefore it allows its citizens easy access to its many fine historical and contemporary cultural institutions.

Since poets and painters receive their ideas from the depths of their souls, Boccia understands creativity to be a spiritual, transcendent process.

Since 1981 he has been published in over fifty journals and has received sixty awards. He is included in five anthologies. Between 1993 and 2008, he had seven chapbooks published.

As for the future, he plans to continue writing and painting.

The Old Man and His Cane

When a small dark room
lives inside an old man
the years breathe time
and time clocks the past
beyond the old man's recall.

When his thoughts turn gray
along the rim of a dream,
and the voice of a wheel
whispers inside him,
the small dark room
gets smaller and darker,
while the old man's eyes cast shadows
of his past.

After he strokes his beard
and licks his lips,
after he stoops to pick up his slippers,
the old man plunges his came
through the room inside him,
wounding beams of ego
and selfish walls
of what was once
a small dark room.

A Confession

Forgive me, I believe a child
was born a bolt of love,

The land was opaque, but not the
skin of the child.

Laugh or cry with me,
I thought I saw in that birth
a meadow peaceful as space
and deeper than hope.

Forgive me my questions
I put to the child,
uncertainties put upon me by friends.

Forgive me my tongue, now
suffering the aftereffects of doubt.

This is not the time to claim
flesh for the soul:

today's hero is making a machine
that shall know itself.
Tomorrow it will say:

forgive me, forgive me my lack
of programmed pain
forgive me, I do not know
how to forgive.

Mary Ann de Grandpre Kelly

Mary Ann de Grandpre Kelly

Mary Ann deGrandpre Kelly has roots in Chicago and Montana, lives in St. Louis, is active in the literary community, and is a board member of St. Louis Poetry Center. She has five children and taught for thirty years in public school. Her poems are in the chapbook *NOTHING SMALLER THAN YOUR ELBOW*, in the 2008 *MARGIE: An American Journal of Poetry*, and she is a James H. Nash Poetry Contest winner. Her plans are to write poems, watch her grandchildren grow, and see the Rocky Mountains again.

Snow Stung

An early thaw
and my cup
of dented tin
scoops
ice melt
from Carpenter Creek.
One sip.

Frost pinches
my nostrils
closed,
chills
my lips,
crystals
my tongue.
The slush
sweet from whitened mountain tips
grips my throat.

The last
keen lash
of winter rime
clangs against
these lungs.

Breathless.
Black night.
Stars race.
Like hot cinders,
snow stings
my face,
shakes my heart.
I'm ricocheted.

Table Talk

The girl is slender, long-haired, a junior
at any High, and at dinner tonight, head down,
she won't say who the boy is, envisioning
the days ahead beyond her mirrored face,
now a ripple in the glass tabletop.
Inside, she's scared. Staring across at her,
the younger sister jabs her finger and blurts,
"Really! I'm DYING. That's the ONLY thing
my friends talked about in math today."

The mother says, "When it arrives... *or*..."
and shrugs. The father interrupts, "More, please,"
holds out his cup, looks away. Uninterrupted,
she reaches for the coffee pot, and, "... listen,
you'll just have to give it up... maybe
a family the doctor knows. Or else—
go to Chicago. They'll do it there. Then
no one here will know." A helpless gesture,
then she nods convincingly. "But, honey,
decide in a hurry." A bedroom radio's on.
Bon Jovi sounds bounce down the stairs.
Nobody's eating and dinner's getting cold.

Karen Smead Mondale

<u>Karen Smead Mondale</u>

Karen Smead Mondale, long-time community activist and retired educator, is a member of the St. Louis Poetry Center and Loosely Identified, the women's poetry workshop. She was the Editor of the *St. Louis Poetry Center Newsletter* from 2004 through 2008. She is published in *Breathing Out*, an anthology released by Cherry Pie Press; the *Mid Rivers Review;* and online publications *Riehlife* and *Winning Writers*. She won Honorable Mention in the James H. Nash Poetry Contest in 2007, 2008, and 2010. She has given poetry readings in the *River Styx* series at Duff's, at Genesis House, the Regional Arts Commission, the Focal Point, and for a charity event held in the Forest Park Golf House.

Joe, 1960 (1937 – 1994)

If he had come knocking at my door
and said
        I'm sorry, did I wake you?
if he had come knocking at my door
and said
        I was thinking about something…
        Can we talk?
if he had come knocking at my door
and said
        nothing
I would have let him in.

As it was
when I opened the door
and he stood there
slouched against the doorframe,
thumbs notched in the front pockets
of his jeans, smile sexing, posing
like a prostitute leans against a streetlight
and said
        Hey sugar – here's your nigga-boy,
I closed the door
went back to bed
and tried to sleep.

When he came knocking at my door
in the morning
and said
        Thank you.
        I just had to know,
I shut the door behind me,
walked into the world with Joe,
aware
that we had been turned inside out
like a dirty shirt tossed into the washing machine
and come out
clean.

Heather Overby

Heather Overby

Heather Overby grew up in Virginia, but lives in St. Louis. She doesn't really know what to do with an M.F.A., but is still not completely okay with law school (sorry, lawyer friends). She tried learning Russian when she visited St. Petersburg in the summer of 2008. Oftentimes, her accent was so awful it would be as though she said "Ilee, are lau ooo?" instead of "Hello, how are you?" Many Russians shook their heads in wonder.

Heather has at least six gigs of music on her computer that she never listens to. She always brings not enough or too many things, wherever she goes.

As a child, she spent a few weeks every summer at her grandparents' farm. While there, she learned: how to shoot a gun; exactly what she is allergic to; that a chicken can totally best a toy poodle in a match of will and strength; that bacon smells like pigdeath; and that, while WWII created many heroes, it did not, exactly, maintain them all.

Overby does not like pants. In this way, she resembles an early twentieth-century teetotaler. Whenever she meets attractive men with rural accents, she imagines for a moment that she could live on a farm full time. This is proven to be untrue. As it was, she barely survived her childhood.

She is currently working on a poem.

What Bears Watching

1.
Things that surface fast, like empty soda cans, dry sponges, anything flesh and blue. I know you wish you could almost float, so put a bit of matter to your tread and take on what rises first.

2.
The darkness with the least light but the most texture. Scream when you feel wool in it.

3.
The corner mouths. Remember to keep your eye on every little corner mouth. Be aware of who they follow with their sly, happed purses. Tag along for the want.

4.
What refuses to unfasten immediately before you, like buds undeceived by early warmth, the doors of just abandoned houses. This is how you approach despair – stomp until you see its smallest petal, until its porch falls in.

5.
Any man willing to place stilts upon his shoulders, who is ready to perch your house upon the stilts. Wait for rain. Hope for fish. Pray for flood.

6.
Any woman bare-spoken as winter, too far gone for wifeliness. Set a jar on her head, a hot on her belly. Pray for fresh wilderness to tame.

7.
The nearest, youngest children. Careful – their smiles are still turned into corners, are only mirrors behind clock hands laughing.

8.
The proper side of the grass. Always mind the bottom side of the grass. Any sea-brink town could tear into a million pieces of tissue paper – become a black and beige heap to dissolve along shoreline. Better to landlock your gaze ahead of time.

9.
The light with so little shadow you forget where to rest your soles, your palms, forget what your throat can do.

10.
Your bright influence. If you cannot go outside a kitchen or a toolbox, just sit and watch what might happen without you.

11.
Sighs that give everything away then ask for too little. Let your lids do the talking. Then give whatever breath you've got left – I'm hungry and the wall's edges offer no more for us.

Amanda Goldblatt

Amanda Goldblatt

Amanda Goldblatt is fairly new to St. Louis and is fairly in love with it. Its underdog scent and embarrassment of parks was the first thing she noticed, followed quickly by the beautiful smiles of St. Louisians as she paced the sidewalks (pacing being a regular pastime of poets and misanthropes) — those things, and the stars of the Walk of Fame (which, it is worth noting, Goldblatt planned to memorize in order – a mission she has since quietly abandoned). When asked recently why she loved St. Louis so much, she flushed and giggled, "I don't know. I just feel creative here."

She is a sheep in wolf's clothing, which is to say that she is a fiction writer who writes poetry. Other fiction writers like to accuse her of being a poet, and poets like to accuse her of being a poet, yet still for some reason she holds dear the bristly gray fur of her beloved wolf suit. It should also be noted that she is allergic to wool. Literally. Lately she has been saying that she is a cross-genre writer, which is a convenient way of saying, "I write what I want to write, wolves and sheep be damned."

Goldblatt's work can be found in *Diagram*, where her story "Girls Who Love Horses" was a finalist for their 2008 Experimental Fiction Contest. "Transmission from the Outpost" was recently published in the debut issue of the women's art and literary magazine *Art XX*. Her story "Her Beard" will be published in a forthcoming issue of *Redivider*. She is currently an M.F.A. candidate at the Washington University in St. Louis Creative Writing Program in fiction and at work on a collection that may or may not include...poetry.

What the Bears are Watching

1.
You. Up behind the hunting placket: a black tarp strung against the gap of two pine boughs. They are wondering why you are there, looking discomfited in a too large orange vest.

2.
The French girl you brought along from the women's college. *Ours* she says. *Ours*. The bears do not know that she is calling their furred hulks into the clearing. They believe she is proclaiming possession, and they imagine her velvet parlour and rolling across her grandmother's loop rug while a fire roars in the background, deliciously unchecked. These are American black bears, after all.

3.
A squirrel's tail switching – boastful and extravagant.

4.
In a past life, a black bear was not a black bear but your great aunt. Your great aunt did not believe in reincarnation. She believed, instead, that gold lamé jackets and jaunty felted berets were appropriate toggery for walks along the property pond. She believed in properly sized finger bowls, and monogrammed thank you notes. Someone thinks as they watch the bear-aunt eviscerate a salmon from the river (shimmering entrails adorning her fuzzy maw): the joke is on her.

5.
Leibniz to Bernoulli, 1698: You fear that matter is composed of that which is not quantitative. I respond, it is no more composed of souls than it is composed of points.

6.
Do you have any additional languages?

7.
A bear walks into his kitchen for breakfast. His bear-wife stands at the sink doing dishes, her paw fur gritty and dripping. She shakes her head: her claws have scratched the ceramic flatware, yet again. The bear-husband remembers the scratch tickets purchased and yet unscratched in his blazer pocket, and smiles.

...Is this a joke?

8.
Your third arm, disconnected and discolored: uniformly bruised black as the darkest river stone and glossy too.

9.
No bears get shot in this poem.

10.
Your ostensibly empty-handed departure. And yet. If a great aunt can become a bear can become a beagle can become a French girl can become a thicket of wild onions in your granddaughter's backyard can become, fractured, fleas on a scalp unscratched, then you can birth a bear, without knowing it, and live quite happily with your bear child ad infinitum.

Michael Castro

Michael Castro

Castro writes, "Born 1945, New York City, P.S. 98, 4th grade wrote 'original paragraphs, invented the bebop people & their bebop language.' J.H.S. 52, introduced to 'all the world's a stage,' George Washington H.S. (G. Dubbs), on cliffs overlooking Harlem River wrote stories set in subway for B.Jordan Pulver, forced to resign campus newspaper over comically critical article that made Faculty Advisor laugh aloud but refuse to publish; S.U.N.Y. at Buffalo during revolutionary sixties, home twenty minutes for Thanksgiving 1963 when news came from mad neighbor Suzanne Wolfe Kennedy shot, America's loss of innocence coincided with my own, by' 67 was demonstrating in Washington, all night vigil on Pentagon steps ringed by troops bayonets unsheathed.

"Worked for NYC Welfare Dept., wrote first poems, songs actually, in Welfare Department Black notebook, Lorca & Dylan my muses; joined caseworker strike for clients rights—then St. Louis, grad school at Washington U. (jumping off point to California?), studied William Carlos Williams & war no more activism, the movement, Peace Eye Poets, first readings coincide with first writings, first book, *Ripple*, with Peace Eye comrades Zelenka, Fleck, Corr; wrote articles & reviews for *St. Louis Outlaw*, corresponded with Allen Ginsberg regarding 'Spontaneous Elegy For Ezra Pound' delivered following news of Pound's death after reading at Webster U, recorded for KDNA & published in *Outlaw 1973*; met Jerome Rothenberg whose anciently rooted ideas of poetry & performance coincided with my own fledging collaborations with musicians of Human Arts Ensemble & Black Artists Group. Brought poetry to St. Louis radio with River Styx Poets (1970-73, KDNA) & cronies Dan Spell, Marvin Hohman, then wife; Jan, show morphed into *River Styx* literary magazine and readings at Duff;s 1975—both still going—many great readings over the years: poetry as communion/community—crossing cultural boundaries— Hung with Ginsberg & other poets & musicians Naropa, centennial summer 1976.,worked with Quincy Troupe throughout the '80s as *River Styx* editors, published *Interpreting the Indian: Twentieth Century Poets & the Native American*, study of Native American influences on American poets (1984), books of poetry *The Kokopilau Cycle (1975), Ghost Hiways & Other Homes (1976), Cracks (1977), (US) (1991), The Man Who Looked Into Coltrane's Horn (1997), Human Rites (2002), The Bush Years (2010).* Hosted *Poetry Beat* radio program, KDHX St. Louis 1989-2003. Poems published in many magazines and anthologies. In 1990's developed poetry performance group Harmony with awesome bards Eugene Redmond, K. Curtis Lyle, Shirley LeFlore, musicians Malik King, J.D. Parran, Gary Sykes, Papa Wright; also began translating modern Hungarian poetry with Gabor G. Gyukics. Collaborations resulted in the anthology *Swimming in the Ground: Contemporary Hungarian Poetry* (2001) and *A Transparent Lion: Selected Poetry of Attila Jozsef* (2006), an as yet unpublished manuscript of great Gypsy poet Attila Balogh, many readings in Budapest, and performances with Hungarian musicians. Years of musical collaborations culminate in recordings with Fred Tomkins Poetry & Music Ensemble ('Freedom Ring,' 2001 and 'Curve Extended,' 2004), Joe Catalano ('Deep Mirror,' 2008), J.D. Parran ('Kokopilau,' 2008), and 'Needle of Light,' with the Human Arts Ensemble 2010.

"Poetry for me, on or off the page, is the central fact of life influencing, shaping everything I do. It is the language beyond language, creation in the largest and smallest senses. It gives speech to the spirit that expands and connects us."

Eighteen Timeless Minutes

that Ann happened to be scrambling by the crevasse
in the cliff at Pueblo Alto
on the day of the solstice

& that she happened to look in
through the slit in the cliff face
down through the earth

& that she happened to see the spiral petroglyph
that no other visitor or worker at the park
had up to then sited,

& that she happened to glance in to the hidden room
at that precise time
during the quadrennial eighteen minute period

when the dagger of sunlight
bisects the spiral form
etched on the flat stone slab far back in time

& that she was the only person in the world
who could have realized & processed that observed
information
& obsessed on it & developed it & understood it

& shared it with everyone else in the world
to the degree that she did,
& that it seemed she had been called

by the light
for that purpose—
the light admitted

by the boulders & rocks
placed so casually as to appear
randomly natural

by Anasazi, they say,
maybe means "old ones,"
no one remembers

the penetrant light
intersecting precisely
the stone slab's spiral's center

solstice & equinox
'sun dagger'
they called it

marking time's
sacrifice

on the sunshaft calendar,
the mysterious spiral
etched on the hidden flat stone slab

& those surface stones
placed above by "Chacoan Einsteins"
just so, to appear random

casually admitting in
the shadow of the moon,

& the nineteen turns of the spiral on the altar
(curved like galaxies & snail shells)
the nineteen turns

traced the moon's journey
in its nineteen year cycle—

strange
unchanging
changes—

quadrennial sunshafts
piercing, dividing

moon shadow creeping
over the labyrinth

turn to turn
round & round moving
further & further in

toward the center
of the spiral
year after year

as the earth
turned

stranger stranger

day & night
sun & moon
above

& below
inside the earth
coiling

on the sacrificial slab

light
penetrating
darkness

where uncoiling snakes
ooze through fissures
darkness to light

*

Ann noted it all & how

in the nineteenth year
when the moon was furthest
from the earth,

its hemispheric shadow
bisected the spiral
perfectly—

& then Ann noticed—

at the solstices that year
with moon & sun
in extreme relation to earth

moon at its furthest, sun its nearest
in the womb-like cleft in the cliff

moonshadow & sundagger
met
& were one

for eighteen timeless minutes
on the stone altar

at the center
of the spiral bed

*

all this recorded
on page & on film
by Ann herself

awed & mystified
at this dance &
this sacrifice

this ritual language
of earth & universe,
of love & light & mind

Obi Nwakanma

Obi Nwakanma

Obi Nwakanma was educated at the prestigious Government College Umuahia, the English-type boarding school where famous Nigerian writers including Chinua Achebe, Christopher Okigbo, Gabriel Okara, V.C. Ike, Elechi Amadi, Ken Saro-Wiwa and many others, went before him. He studied English at the University of Jos in Nigeria, got his M.F.A. at the Washington University in St. Louis, and received a Ph.D. in English at Saint Louis University, St. Louis, Missouri.

Nwakanma is considered among the most influential of contemporary Nigerian poets and writers. His collection of poems, *The Roped Urn* was awarded Nigeria's prestigious ANA/CADBURY prize for poetry. He is also the recipient of the Walter J. Ong Award for distinguished achievement in 2008. He has worked as a journalist in Nigeria; as Group Literary Editor of the *Vanguard* and the Deputy Editor and columnist on *Sunday Vanguard* where he continues to write a weekly column, "The Orbit" on Sundays, on politics, culture, and international affairs. He has corresponded for *Newsweek* magazine, the *Neue Zurcher Zeitung* of Zurich and *Independent* in South Africa. He has also completed the biography of the famous Nigerian poet, Christopher Okigbo, who died fighting in Biafra in 1967, due out by James Currey Publishers, Oxford, in 2009.

His latest book of poems, *Horsemen & Other Poems* was published by the Africa World Press, New Jersey (2007). He is also currently at work on a novel and a play. He teaches Creative Writing and Literature of the Black Diaspora at Truman State University, Kirksville, Missouri.

Indigo Street

i.

There... there, crags and boulders –
Who know about them, but the wayfarer?
The Alps, the whiteflag, imperceptible footprints

Who knows –

Friend, the jags blunted by the cloud, the swelling
Of shoals in the sacred heart of river
Through which we may return?

ii.

Now, a calm settles
Over the spilth
Of incandescent day –

The day is a quilt

Made from renewals: vivid Elysium, our
Cities woven out of air. Bracken. Records
Of frayed names, Genghis –
Anukili –
A museum of learning: I have
Brought disorders to Cathay; I
Have found three gods washed ashore;
They died a mean death. Under their
Hooked jaws, four times fixed with strings,
A tale of the slain beast, glared out of the lens:

I have crossed the river homeward, and
You might as well know, to remember us,
That do not draw the lot, or pay our tithes –
Or scrutinize our names on passports –

Impartial foretellers of wrecked journeys.

We have hatched anew, under the sharp eyes of
falcons,
Who test our DNA for illicit sex, perhaps even the
terrorist gene –
A dognose, a pure sign of the wetlands, the delta or
island
Of tutelary gnomes, the caballero, a Spanish
onslaught,
Braving the Southwind, heading towards the smoke
of Santa Isabella
And the ruin of Port au Prince.

iii.

One day we crouched under the flowerbeds, running
From the deep wisdom of science, and the
Guile of politics; hiding from the tax collector,
From the immigration squad, and missing the point –

The arched, and the precise humour
Of the city police: we hid under the palce silence
Of the faceless, riding the tube in London & Paris,
New York is like the lion's claw after 9:11; just
Before the truculent purrs of the city cats, the
Cur, the purr of the jaguar at the street's corner –

Just before the pubs open, to the pubic pressure
Of working men: we are faceless among the city
lights,
The reticent manners of identity, with its birth
certificates
And occupancy permits, the humble things that grow
cold
With coffee, and with age –

May we enquire, sire, the next time the train will
run?

Or accept this trifling token, my unspoken
compliment
Stranger; your well-bred and courteous manner, your
voluble
Speech, your homemade dignity, your expensive
snort
Near Wall Street, is a symptom of abstinence.

Or absence sir. The subaltern, he makes a jug of
lemonade,

And hawks desire in teaspoons. It may be providence
That furnishes me with a quick appetite; sir, scratch

My rockets and you will find thunder.

Thunder screwed the Moor. The matron. The bride.
All saw their pride stolen. It was thunder that spoke
In tongues. The urgent crisis. The verbosity, sir, the
gross

Atrocity! The sly fellow seeking integration –

iv.

Speaking of which, I now stop
With dignified tears, to say to the
Commission of Human Rights: look, look

To Odi, and Umuechem:
Bring the criminal Cat to book
And I will return with evidence;
With a steady stare: but with a million dead

At the Cablepoint alone;
And only silence mark their graves,
With the fog still clinging to the water,
& whetstones hissing again –

The grim onslaught is a mere sign:
The river, they say, now belches poison: shall
We then consider the evidence? No one was left
In the village. They went to dance and to
Their deaths. Came five months later in a squat
cavern –
Shell BP struck, seventy fathoms in daily drums:

The water rose. Yours lovingly, with a pickaxe,
With four lads on a narrow track; with the
Ingot in their eyes, burnt the Niger bridge.

What time is the next train sir?

v.
Darling –
I found some work today
But I am still incomplete
                              My papers, that is: incomplete.
But now I have a number.
A green card. A residence permit. In town, young men
Stare at me. Some have choked on my name.
Some amused at the bent of my speech. Your accent:
The waitress said, wrapping fish & fries, ten cents
Less for me: your accent: where is that from?
Haiti?
You with twisted locks: do you know Tosh?
Are you here to stay?
Did you grow up very poor?
Are you loving it here?

A sharp western light pours through my window –
Silver blades studded with diamonds of memory;
Of you my land, my all, my day wreathed
With palms: on Palm Sunday, accurate hips swayed
& sang under tousled hair. My dear,
carnivals, the hayride, downtown petals slough
off season; from Broadway, a harsh pigment, Heroin, poignant,
by the Meeting of the Waters, spouting pure venom, in front of
the old Union Station, now turned Omni; I throw a salute
to my countryman, the cabdriver, the Eritrean, or the Senegalese doorman –
the Calabari, the ebb of migrants into the sewage; the underground –
the blank fringe fading to a pause: I found work, I said,
in Iron-mongery, assistant to the nightwatch, an old Ukrainian doctor,
now doctoring the minutes, and in silence sit,

over homemade syrup, and starlight filtering from
sea to sea.

I have found a home among complete poems;
Madrigals, crack cocaine bury my reels
Of fruitless Septembers. There are no autumns in my
past,
Nor winters in my antiquity; love is scarce and the
tax is
High; the capital is disproportionate; I
Have sold the jewels you gave me; my name
Etched on it –

I have heard rumours from home, love,
In the last two months that have run amok,
Of strong winds mixed in strong drinks;
But I have remitted only bile though Western Union,
The tax is high –

Everything fluttered around the burnt city; the rest
Hang free – like me – unrooted; Housni the
Moroccan, offered me hashish and dates, and
Sufi chants on CD-rom;

And Hafiz –

O horses O horses of memory
Ride me, spread your hooves
Over these stony paths, where
My frayed breadth lie aghast
Over the price of distance. And of sugar –

The tax is high –

For we counted in Florissant, a high number
Of the lost. I live in a walled place, you
Should see me now: high on Apple cider and
Gingerbread;

I fear calories in regular food; I have registered with the Green Party
And a good co-op, for organic mild from Vermont. I have stopped taking you
Phonecalls. They rouse me up at 5:00am. It must be lunchtime
Nigerian time; even here, the times have gone crazy:
We counted in Hazelwood,
A high number –

vi.
My brother, Courage,
Read Winthrop
& found nothing of himself
in his wilderness –

So what is America to me?

The same story angling intertwined?
The unreconciled cry from a charred hearth?

For I still swear by the market denizens:
But whom shall I claim as forebear?

The puritans or the Quakers
Who hold everything to the light,
Or to their muse, silence?

To each a handful of earth,
To bury their past and plant a future:

We unrooted the four stones from the
Copses: we no longer offer wine or yam, & the first
Yield of the earth; we are very modern –
We eat of the cannibal broth: the Eucharist,
The blood of Jesus –
We call him father – the exile from Ur –
Jah-Jehovah's main man.

But when is the next train sir?

To Schenectady, to Rindge, to Ithaca
& Syracuse – where is Amawbia on the map?

And the nerve of it, stranger. The moss glistening by its season,

The circus, mister, the adder in the hands of the magus;

And what nerve you have, to disturb my universe;
To unsettle the settled.

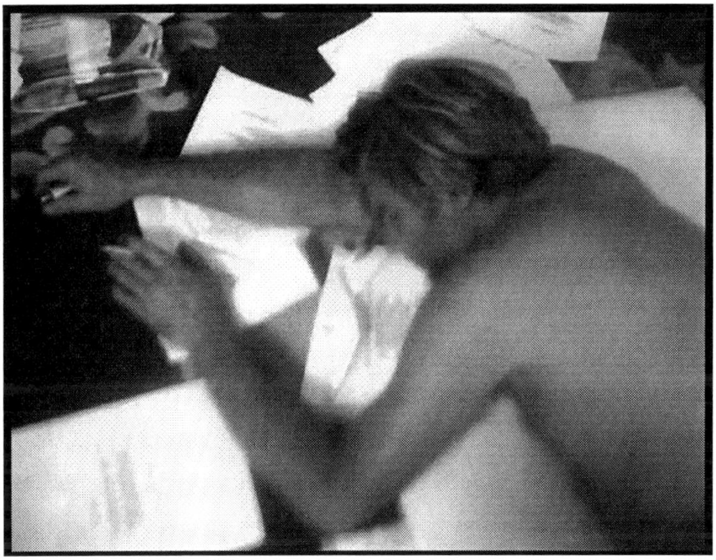

Kenneth L. Brown

Kenneth L. Brown

Born in Missouri- left town at nineteen...Returned twenty-one years later after Minnesota, Maine, and Mississippi in a tent,

Montana, Morocco- where he lived with a prostitute afflicted with polio. Normandy, Madrid, Grecian Islands- despondent- to upstate New York across the country in a Honda- through

Mexico- Vegas- Santa Monica for four years doing laundry for a living then dog-sitting at the Ding Dong,,,Wound up in

Australia-Perth- the out-bush for nine months- Hell's Angels- blew up land- went broke- made ten thousand dollars on Karma Kards- fell in love for the thirteenth time- engaged-

Kicked out of Australia- published in 45 periodicals- wound up back where he started.

You're a Whore Now

Cars criss crossing caustically –
you're never gonna be my friend.
As a matter of fact I hope you croak:
It's all based on the Zen of when…

And why were you so silent
after showing me resilience?
Your greed, your need for getting
what you think you're worth
is less than ken.

Your promises, like vomit,
were like rockets in my pocket.
I offered you a future: You said yes…
But where was virtue?

You're a vulture.
Where was culture?
I'm a statue, yes,
but you're a whore now.

She Seemed to Like Me

I screwed and unscrewed light bulbs for her,
dusted cobwebs out the corners,
hand-scooped clean her muddy gutters,
swept Styrofoam and feathers into dustpans;
hosed her entire car park down
with double rhythmic pulsing nozzles –
squirted the floor she walked on
and swabbed up afterwards.

Oedipus Rex Had a Complex Complex

Be careful not to cover
every angle
of life's contradictions...

You'll wind up
weeping bitterly
on the sheets
your dead mom
fucked on.

Catherine Rankovic

Catherine Rankovic

Catherine Rankovic, M.F.A., is the author of *Fierce Consent and Other Poems* (2005), *Island Universe* (2007), and *Meet Me: Writers in St. Louis* (Penultimate Press, 2010) a collection of in-depth interviews with 13 St. Louis writers. She has lived in St. Louis since 1988 courtesy of its low rents, high culture, and gemlike literary community -- a cluster of writers comparable, she insists, to the one in Paris in the 1920s, and she's thinking ahead to the day when everyone will know that. Her poetry and prose have appeared in *River Styx, Boulevard, Gulf Coast, The Iowa Review, The Missouri Review, Natural Bridge*, and several anthologies including *Are We Feeling Better Yet? Women Speak About Health Care in America* (Penultimate Press, 2008). She is an adjunct professor of English at Washington University.

People Are Flowers

My grandfather called me a flower once. – *Frank D.*

Free to approach us, each face
a full bloom with tiny
or mammoth eyes and lashes,
crowns and ruffs, all
ranges of petaldom, mouths
vicious or vacuous, they roam,
at bus stops balance coins
on leaf tips; shy as roses
or like marigolds bold and hatless,
    they choose their own tints,
arrange themselves in public fountains,
taste rivers and runoff,
are rapt at our questions, pleased
and the more vivid when stared at.
Attracted to trellises,
loving and hating only
the weather, aware that
emotions will not injure them,
    they breathe in what we breathe out,
like friends. They swell on graces
prepared for them.
They marvel.
With dry eyes they seed
the world to follow.
The heads they carried
as parasols, grow light and hollow.

Gourds

Among the frail green bean vines,
beneath the leaves, so that when we harvested beans
we were surprised, grew these
    polymorphs: long-necked, pot-bellied, hard-
shelled
marigold-orange and bile-green cysts,
    hanging gaily and perversely from the trellis,
hanging in the air like an accordion notes.
Each witty but poker-faced, as if
it had just cracked a joke and was feigning
innocence, waiting for our stupefaction
to give way so we could see we were its
godparents and goats, as we were for the zucchini
that, hidden in shadows, bulked so hugely,
we left it at the door of a church
with a note saying we couldn't take care of it.
In the change-pocket of the earth
gourds are the nickels and slugs that won't fit:
curcubits
inedible as socks, good for nothing
but rue and amusement. "Don't
crack these open, or the seeds will sprout."
"How'd they get in there?" How whimsical, cute,
these ugly callused children of the harvest;
ugly art, intended to exact
only curiosity about the artist –
spun up from what impulse? Whose? To laugh?
Who brought the seeds here on the bottom of his
shoe?
What are they for, these misbegotten
bad-example fruits,
when dried out good only for maracas
as raspy and Latinate and tasteless
as genitalia when they're not in use?

Katy Miller

Katy Miller

Katy Miller was born in St. Louis. She attended Vanderbilt University in Nashville, Tennessee, and received a B.A. in English. Katy then lived for five years in Washington, D.C. She moved back to St. Louis to pursue her Masters in Social Work at Washington University.

Does she like it here? Yes, most of the time.

What does she think about poetry? Being from the Midwest, I have a hunch there is something highfalutin' about sharing too many thoughts about poetry. Whatever I write now, I would probably read in a couple years and decide it was irritating. That being said, after three years of writing poetry and a lifetime of reading it, it doesn't lose its wonder and pleasure for me.

How come she writes? It is the only means of creative expression, so far it appears, I've been blessed with. My singing voice is terrible and I can't seem to draw either.

Has she been published before, received any awards? My work has appeared in *Margie*, Volumes, 6, 7, and 8. I was a winner of the St. Louis Arts in Transit 2008 Poetry in Motion contest. More poems are forthcoming in *Pleiades* and the *American Journal of Nursing*.

What are her plans for the future? I would like to publish a poetry book that would hopefully include some of the poems I wrote based on my experience as a hospice social worker. I also plan to continue learning about poetry and writing, and raising my children.

Unlearning

If you possess the longevity for it, you will know the deconstruction of everything.

It's ocular the way it happens,
as if someone wiped your eyes clean,
the great baby that you are.
You wail and squawk, incredulous.
Everything you read, everything you see,
even a picture as true as a photograph
you know to be counterfeit.

It's mechanical the way it happens,
as if a wrench turned a fact counterclockwise,
dissembling parts.
The fact, as true as a family,
in pieces and exposed as merely a belief.

It's magical the way it happens,
as if Oz were your home and
Kansas a dream.
In Oz you love and are beloved,
but it's a spell cast on you.
You are sent back to the place you've never been:
Kansas, where everything is solid,
made of nothing but ground.

It's medicinal the way it happens,
as if the elixir were not ingested,
but a great baptism.
You are submersed,
dissolving in it.

Brett Underwood

Brett Underwood

Brett Lars Underwood flew here through the dust of cornfields with a broken wing and a head full of ideas. He was immediately snatched up by a doctor's daughters and bi-polar musicians. After walking across town a thousand times and riding in convertibles through the North Side with entrepreneurs oblivious to psilocybin, he has decided to stay, despite the fact that the doctor's daughters and many more women have departed. The bipolar musicians either killed themselves or are still in his acquaintance.

Once upon a time, he co-published a 'zine entitled *LICK MY SQUAGGLE NOOSE, CLAM TICK.* That venture may have led to him being published in other 'zines that you haven't heard of and definitely paid the rent at Kinko's for a month or two. He has written Zen koans for *The Riverfront Times* and *St. Louis Magazine* and described the scoring and defense of many high school and American Legion sporting events for various journals of suburbia. Most recently, his work has been featured in *52nd City* (http://52ndcity.com).

Underwood is somewhat of a gadabout and busy body and as such was awarded a Kick-Ass Award in 2006, but it had little or nothing to do with his poetry. It had something to do with his organization of the annual Day of the Dead Beats reading and his now deceased-radio show on KDHX, *The No Show.*
In the future, Underwood plans to walk back and forth on rubber mats and spill drinks for money. Failing that, he may take a bicycle ride.

Sometimes I Work in a Grandiose Castle

Standing on clouds of epiphanies
the rush of the hungry and the damned
washed away
I stop and look out the aged
windows to the world

Wonder what it's like to look in
at the light
the calmly dining
public

Them
free from the streets
locked away from danger

Hunger
and the mad rush for goods.

Out there
Snow falls silently
on barren branches that
never bear fruit
but only sticks of leaves
void of nourishment
only serving to break
up the asphalt beds of
the commuting damned

A vagrant few pass through
alleys behind the blockaded
forts of the captains of industry
and I am safe to observe
in the warmth of perusal
under pillars and beams of long since
slaughtered cedars

I imagine that I am seated
near one of those small saplings
out there

In a simple wooden chair
sipping cheap bourbon or
other distilled and warming spirits
The wind and cold no challenge
as I look in and see
myself
with scorn
standing behind my altar of
refined leisure
each sip melts the hatred

Until another order for urgency
makes itself known
in the form of shrieking and
harried voices
both human and electronic
To the clacking of credit
cards on the bar
My feet turn to glass
as the clouds on which I was
wondering
shoot needles of sleet into my mind

The calm faces turn to those of
ghouls
with gnashing teeth
and hungry, blood-sucking
souls
the chupacabra have
come

I am not sweating
The small stuff
I'm bleeding minutiae
out my eyes

But
It is time to make due
until I can wonder why
such precious still moments
are few

Or moments like these
when I can
get them down
out of a fuzzed
attic space

Just now, I've returned from a quick
few drags on the back porch
during a warm break from
Winter

The birds are chirping stupidly
as a church bell rings
But a generator is growling
at the end of an alley
from a building being rehabbed
in the name of real estate
Renovation
Commerce
and the good of the city

I know I'm lucky to have such
easy disturbances
like yipping schnauzers
clomping neighbors
on wooden steps
and the banging and clanging
of carpentry
free from Jesus

But I can't help to feel their
encroachment as threatening
while a taxi's horn blares
for the fat lady to
waddle down for her ride to
somewhere else

and the clock catches my eye

Soon I'll be returning to the trenches
to fight off these fears of aging
To loosen myself from
the nooses of debt
to free myself for more
easy moments
as the future yawns uncertainly
Stretching its jaws for its next meal
languid and waiting for its
soon-to-come easy gruel
of we
the restless
on a Saturday night
Easing ourselves down
into the belly of the beast
A mad rush
for more of the good, dirty
funnish Hell.

Marilyn Probe

Marilyn Probe

Marilyn Probe was born in St. Louis, with roots so deep, extending to the Ozarks, she will never leave. On the Meramec, she plucks lines beneath unfettered stars at night and swims against the river current to observe herons and barn swallows. She writes to understand who she is.

Probe's poetry is often on natural, spiritual, and narrative themes, features primarily women, and are published in anthologies such as *Breathing Out, Poems by Loosely Identified* and *New Harvest: Jewish Writing in St. Louis,* and *Nothing Smaller Than Your Elbow*. She has published in literary journals such as *Big Muddy, The Kerf, Mid-Rivers Review, Oasis 2007, CAJE Nat'l. Journal, Messages From the Heart*, Washington University's *Figure in the Carpet*, and *Missouri Library World.* A recent outreach chair and board member of the St. Louis Poetry Center, she has garnered James H. Nash Awards. She was a Poetry Society of America, Metro Arts in Transit Poetry in Motion and American Society on Aging Poetry Contest winner. She uses humor as well as forms and free verse.

With Teeth in the Earth

I am who I want to be, nourished
by vibrations, humming.
I press my cheek to the hyacinths
to feel the touch of lavender,
inhale the goodness, arousing
the day. My lips hug the earth
and I know love.

My nose steals a scent
and I know joy.
Anyone who digs teeth into the earth
knows roots of passion,
If I must pull away from earth,
not spend days singing its melodies,

with garlic sprouting from last season,
the roses launching the parade,
arugula regrown at sunrise,
the daffodils opening their labia,
and the tarragon displaying silky ruffles,
I would weep in my crumpled bed,
a sterile room, cut off from earth.

Though I could still see the black birds
fleeting home by thousands,
puncturing the ground,
and the shadow of the purple finch
flitting on the bluff bricks
beside the tips of the Austrian pine.

Long Shore Drift

Cataracts ripening, cracks widening, days
diminishing, while time shifts swiftly
as a wild waterfall, not a river. If I had to pick one,

racing forward or long shore drift, I'd choose
the latter. The jewel of solitude sharpening
seas of dreams, a brimming smile, an inside light

never shaded, a seaworthy foot that arches with
grace,
an ocean of abundance no matter how much I
give.
Being in charge of my own helm, no
matter

how the ship's wheel is blasted – tracing
the circular waves of years, the young
might see as parallel lines that never converge.

A ladder to nowhere that shines
like polished brass, and pounding experienced.
Years level the rough edges of quartz

like the blood stream bevels the heart. To age
and release the necessity to reshape the world, to
wrap
as an aquatic snail in a spiral of love,

is a tide worth the waiting
and lessens the tug of the moon,
softens the sound of fear.

Steven Schreiner

Steven Schreiner

"I'm not from St. Louis, but in my twentieth year here I might say I am 'of' St. Louis. I feel about my relationship to place much the way the first realtor I met when I came here felt: 'I came here and I hated it, and seventeen years later I can't leave. It's home.' Except that I always want to leave, until I get home from a trip or even from a day at work. I've lived in the city, which I loved, despite the high cost of what my neighbor, whose home was in the 8000 square feet of the first firehouse in St Louis, called 'country club dues.' We had these wonderful brick edifices, in a historic location, we could smell the brewery every day, and we owned it all on the cheap; but there were industrial menaces like the company at the foot of our alley that repaired truck trailers all through the night; there were robberies of just about everything, including my hedges and my potted plants; and there were the best and worst of neighbors, sane and demented, who made life interesting night and day. Everything was brick. In my county cottage the trees are elegant enough to stave off longing for a new place one day at a time. In the sweeping winds that sometimes clear the air of this valley town, I gaze up at my oaks and stand rooted.

"Writing is everything in this town. There are more writers than you can count, more readings, more fame, more classes, more workshops, more visitors, more book signings, more to do of a literary nature than is possible to do. The talent pool is immense. Those who climbed from the pool—T. S. Eliot, Marianne Moore, Tennessee Williams—is rivaled only by those who changed music and who came from the banks of this river. It's sick how much is going on here.

"The schools are a big part of it: four universities within the city limits, a few more beyond its limits, and a community college system held in high regard. It's a teaching town, even if the state can't get its act together to fund public education at a higher tax rate than at least forty-five other states; still, many subsist on teaching here, many more seek learning from these great professionals, and many make it through the ranks out of these schools. I haven't done much but go to school most of my life, so it's fine with me to work in one. I'm lucky to do so. It's my great good fortune."

Silk

I chose the flowers quickly
the day I came to see you,
home from the hospital,
your baby on your breast,
and I waited downstairs until
I was asked for. I didn't wish
to see you like that, wearied,
torn, your clothes disarrayed
as though a storm swept through
and you – and *this* – remained.
Arriving in the room, I saw
from a distant door I once
had called my own, you there
in the corner far away and small.
I thought to see, when my eyes sharpened
in the window light
to shut out all I couldn't
take, the father, lounging in silk.
He slept on in the next room
and you were as you were. For you
waiting in my arms as if I carried
the cut-down, tendered blooms
across a rain swell or a wave
washed ashore from wherever
the unwanted go or come back from,
the vivid, foolish, clown-faced daisies,
the course, lumescent, faintly ghoulish
metallic petals of the eucalyptus.

The Snow

Now they're collecting the snow
we awaited so expectantly
and for which we have only one word.
Here we do not say snow before nightfall,
wet snow of rush hour, snow
like new dimes or snakes on a dry highway,
snow like cake
rising on the branch,
unforgiveable spring snow
burning magnolia blossoms, shivering
in the throat of a crocus, snow that hurts
the eyes, that makes you want to turn
away, snow that falls on the tongue
of the ocean,
snow that squeaks, snow that whispers,
that no longer stirs the limbs
of lovers, snow of parting
falling on two, one lonely
and one in love with snow,
crazy snow circling around
like a father who can't find his child,
that makes the night too bright
to sleep; inconsolable
snow that falls upon
a widow's veil and melts
as she walks from the garden
of stone, snow
that makes the night a negative,
snow on her already
purchased plot, snow in the grove
of flameless cedars.

One kind of snow to be dispensed with
the day after.

After the Rain

Everything is wet
this morning after the rain.
The needles of the white pine
are fattened with drops
like beads along a string.
Now a wind passes over
waking the old oaks
and it sounds like rain
returning. I remember
when young
summer days, how bored
I was yet happy
that we could not work
on the wet wood
of a half-framed house.
At home, between semesters,
the weight of your story
not yet upon me,
only the one love,
and nearness to death
still a joke
full of feeling
like a dare,
I'd wait for the rain
to let up
and it would return
wave upon wave
as if it were tireless
or unsatisfied.
I've known desire
once, maybe more
than once, to feel
like that, and I've held on
for its return.
It's here again
now that I'm waiting
for you, and for you

and for you, the lost love,
the impossible love
and the uncreated one,
which is only this
thing I say now.
Who would care?
The red leaves of the maple
under the lens of the sun
through the bright water
are not red at all,
more like a child's finger
held to a flashlight
almost flayed, as when
you come upon hunger
and its work in the woods.
The air is that of a sea
coast, just above the waves,
whitened with a bright mist
so that the birds, too,
are whitened, bleached
of detail, an Aegean
whiteness, except for the trees
drenched and heavy.

When the rain lifted
there was the next day's
work to worry about
and the refusal to love
anything. The wet lumber
squeaked with nails
and squirted when the hammer
hit and there was silence
most of the day. I remember
the smell of sugar
and amber, of pulp
and the darkened sap
of knots, the weight
of plywood against my shoulder
and palm as I climbed

the ladder to the bare roof
and laid it down
relieved of fear, then
did it again. So much
for the white dress
of a summer bride
and her hair woven
with rain. Afternoons
asleep on the sofa
for an hour after work,
I'd wake and cry out
for my life, certain
I'd missed the day.

Colleen McKee

Colleen McKee

How did you wind up in St. Louis? Do you like it here? I was born illegitimate in a hospital named after a broken heart. I moved over thirty times by age eighteen, due to confusion, poverty, and a variety of crises, but always within Missouri. I stayed in many cabins, shacks, trailers, apartments, and once, an all-metal house. Magnets stuck to the walls. When I was fifteen, I moved in with a petty drug dealer in my first home in the city, in Dogtown, which was actually a nice neighborhood, despite people like us. Later I gravitated to the South Grand area, where every manner of working-class weirdness is acceptable. That's where I belong.

What do you think about poetry? Why do you write? Carving poems into my desk in high school was an absorbing way to avoid the monotony of teachers' voices and the brutality of big-haired girls during the Reagan/Bush era. I haven't really changed that much; now I sit around with my chums drinking beer at CBs and writing on the picnic tables on the patio. The difference is that poetry is rarely a way of escaping my reality now. I usually use it to understand my reality more deeply. I understand the world better when I write about it, which is not to say I understand this world that well. I am a blunt and direct person who believes poetry should communicate with other human beings in a human way. Philosophical reasons aside, I can also think of two practical benefits of writing: Poetry can occasionally be an effective way to get someone cute to kiss me. More often, it is just something to do on the bus.

Have you been published? Won any awards? Of course, I'm so brilliant. I published a collection of poetry about food and sex, *My Hot Little Tomato* (Cherry Pie, 2007). I also co-edited, with Amanda Stiebel, an anthology of personal narratives, *Are We Feeling Better Yet? Women Speak About Health Care in America* (PenUltimate, 2008). Additionally, I have published in *Under the Arch: St. Louis Stories, Bellevue Literary Review, Poetry Daily*, and a variety of other anthologies, journals and websites. I won first place in the Wednesday Club contest, and Arts in Transit award, and other prizes.

What are your plans for the future? I am working on a book of poems called *The Contortionist*, which is about my friend Miko and the peculiar kind of grief, love and questions that follow suicide. What else will I do in the future? I'm sure I will continue to teach writing. Other than that, my only plans are spiritual: to try to be a kind, enjoyable, and useful person.

Love Poem on the 70 Grand

1.

I drift, wake and drift on the bus. The sun
warms my coat on the way to Grand Station:

a city of brick, bricks that shine green
as moss underwater, bricks

like blocks of blood,
of tarnished gold, white clay

bricks stacked high
above black walnut trees.

2.

Pigeons shimmy in the copper gutters
on the roof of the Peveley Dairy, croon in the winter
sun.

When they cross the street through sky,
their shadows cool my cheek.

3.

My lips taste of butter, habanero, and salt, the scent
of oil in your hair, a kiss

at the scar on your temple,
your morning smile like milk.

"Delmar Station, Arriving, Delmar Station"

O city of soot and lilies,
Here I sit on your white bench.

It's six a.m., and I'm wondering
Why the talking cure won't take.

A man strolling along the platform
Stops – just to say to me – Smile!

I said, "Ever said that to a man?"
I said, "Yeah, I didn't think so.

Once a man broke my heart at a bus stop.
He said he couldn't see me anymore

As his blue eyes stared past my shoulder,
Looking out for the Delmar-McKnight.

I sliced my heart into a poem,
Dada style." The man said, What? I explained,

"Collage. I make valentines
Out of old valentines.

I use dirty chewing gum
And old grocery receipts. By the way,

The lady who draws my blood,
Her name is – *Velva Valentine.*"

"No shit," he said.
"No shit. I slice my brain into squares

And play Scrabble with them.
I have an X, and a Y, and a Z, and a Q,

In other words, I don't know what to do.
Years of analysis, and I am still myself."

I looked up, saw only tickweed
Shivering along steel tracks.

Jessica L. Freeman

Jessica L. Freeman

Jessica L. Freeman has been an artist for many years. She began dancing at the age of six and writing poetry at the age of twelve, after stealing a book of poems from her older brother's bedroom. She was a double major of dance and poetry at Columbia College Chicago and the University of New Mexico in Albuquerque. She currently lives in St. Louis, where she attends Webster University.

Magnetic Ice for Scott and Josh

The sky

Tilted and

I rose saying

Death is time

And time is a

Red Dream Flooded

Yellow #11

A tragic day but I praise you anyway
That I am a sister
Not just to you but to her too
And for all that I love I say
Bring your darkness
Grasp me and hold on
I give over my light always for you and
I beat my breast –its wind
I'm filled with after all
You only see me at funerals
When I'm there
It's my bit I do -to act like a landscape
I never remember that I love you
Or Dogtown, I won't forget all that I needed
Your not music and your not discretions
I won't live in your middle
Your bell
Dour
Its dirt and sky
You sound so loud

Untitled

You are a mountain
    strong and green
I am resting and broken

Tracheluim- The Absurdities of War

At night the sky that is there
Is of solidarity
Expansive and light
  we are trees munching on your bellows
Intrinsic for you, a voice
What will become of you
A recalascent road aroused and burdened that
Moans and mourns for you
We burnt the glass
You made for us
The birds that wobble past
Your doorstep
Its night there is a sky
A fire frozen in your window
The dancing worms you stole for me

Niki Nymark

Niki Nymark

Niki Nymark is a native St. Louisan and a graduate of St. Louis University with degrees in English, Urban Affairs, and Social Work.

She has published several books of poetry, including *Kavannot, A Stranger Here Myself* and *Nothing Smaller Than Your Elbow*, the last with fellow poets Marilyn Probe, Mary Ann deGrandPre Kelly, and Marlene Miller.

Her work also appears in anthologies, *Across the Long Bridge, New Harvest: Jewish Writing in St. Louis 1998-2005, OASIS 2007* and *Gems from the Past: Poetry and Prose Anthology.*

Augusta Anne

Long ago,
Augusta Anne and I
played all summer long,
jumping on round
bales of hay in the barn.
Everything smelled
of chicken feathers

Augusta Anne
stayed a little girl,
eight or nine in overalls
or dimity for church.
When I grew up,
went away to school,
she was still
lying on her belly by the pond
stirring up the tadpoles,
thoughtfully.

"Why don't you grow up?"
I asked her once,
just curious, not mean.
She squinted at me, then
at the sun, "This is just
who I am," she said,
"never saw no sense to it."

Myra South

Myra South

Myra South lives a simple life in a small house surrounded by herbs and flowers. She writes, cooks and paints –

chops onions, carries water –

tells stories, feeds friends and avoids ugliness.

She finds art in the hands of gardeners and woodworkers.

The Iris Liberation Front

We marched with our horticultural artillery,
spades at the ready, clever hand tools
made for lifting things to freedom—
unidentified rhizomes barely visible
beneath a crust of dappled dirt.

We stab and dig and lift
beneath the sword-shaped leaves
cut down by the developer's
hired mowers, oblivious
to Ruby's years of care.

We imagine the missing blooms
the spring palette of colors
unfolding in old fashioned
unnamed strains, mingled over time
and waiting for their rescue.

We parade the stolen flowers back
in my rusty red wagon, destined
to carry moss rose one more summer,
this mission the most it's ever traveled,
carrying the iris to new soil.

Mary Eden

Mary Eden

At seventeen, Mary Eden's eyes opened to a world extraordinarily different than that of her South St. Louis parochial school and church, which she had known since the age of two. Leaving the church and stepping out into this world of wonderment and difference, she began her studies as a student of life.

As the young and informed are obligated, she took advantage of many opportunities for experience through mischief and personal growth, ultimately leading her to responsibility. Eden soon discovered that the same beauty once felt by the faithful survived reality, and she saw the animating and creative forces alive and flourishing in all things. Personal vision ablaze, she was now connected to the city; it was home.

In her formative years, Mary's love for the fine arts shone through in her ever blossoming ability to create. English and creative writing grabbed hold, fascinating her mind and focusing her talents. From her first journals at the delicate age of ten flowing through now, her poetry is an emerging detail in the foreground of the infinite "big picture." She pulls from her authorial voice to deny fear, stare down failure, to learn, to be aware, harvest the wind, fight the tide, beat the drain.

In active pursuit of her craft, Eden has ventured to the odd poetry reading and art seminar alike and is much honored to be a part of this, her first formal publication. The future holds the fruits of her journaling past organized in what will be a semi-autobiographical account of what it is to come of age, post-millennium, arriving as a kid and existing as lower-middle class working woman.

The Collector

to gurgling sinks and suction,
here lies this- how it always was,
at the merciful countertop,
where it only took ten square years
to figure out that you're not watched, asshole.
funny, she says, how it's easier to be alone
among a room of strangers
than to be estranged in a room of your own.
be still, my chuckling heart.
here we have the human race,
and they're off.

Score And Four

ouch-cracked neck cramping, i'm stretched tense.
please, no, not another aspirin.

just give me the green stimulation,
'cause laughter is a much more worthwhile auto-
distract.

glued to the glass fruit case
of our friend the BBC,
onto the flipping-burger fish-popping circus
of spatulas and tongs and dripping ladles.

we are the grease, and it is the word,
and the word was always with grease,
and it always was grease.

what do real people do?

Godspell

oh, the concept of undeniable, unwavering heterosex.
through what fingers have I slipped?
alpha male or female?
beta anti-form?
gamma absence?
delta void?
before me now, the venus de milo also asks,
pauses,
finally responds, "clearly not mine."
so we in haste make the david?
what has he for the centuries?
the non-presence of a well deserved leaf!
"we beseech thee! HEAR us!
come sing about love!"
-I knew it.

Mathieu Paul

Mathieu Paul

Mathieu Paul was born and raised on the south side of St. Louis, but spent five days out of seven in a rust-stripped trailer in Imperial, Missouri. Paul was learned in the St. Louis Public School System, so he's not very smart. He began working forty-plus hours per week when he was sixteen and is now extremely tired. In January 2007, he released a split chapbook with Joseph Sulier, under the title *Get Born*, which has become a writers' collective, showcasing the talents of various St. Louis and traveling writers by holding multiple monthly readings and releasing chapbooks of their work. You can check him out on Facebook or at www.myspace.com/getbornbeat. Paul can be reached at mathieu-incognito@hotmail.com

Frenchy

Frenchy flew the coup. Spread them white feathered wings & set soaring out my bedroom window this morning. I should have seen it coming but I never even saw her go. All the others have stayed till I'm wide awake walking them out the front door. This is why I told Joe when he asked why I said No to advances from the mad young gal we both know, I says to him I says, "I didn't want to wake up next to her. Mornings like that can make a man loathe the scent of jasmine..."

Not Frenchy though, oh no, she's the type of gal you want to wake up next to. When you fall asleep in her arms you will dream of watching her rise, watching her wipe the sleep out her eyes, yawning, stretching one hand to the Lord perking small soft breasts braless beneath a black spaghetti strap.

There I lie though, too drunk to be dreaming, just passed out grinding my teeth. She boarded her bicycle bound for deceit leaving me sprawled naked beneath my crimson sheet on her old bed. I awoke feeling as though I had a wooden stake driven deep into my heart. Frenchy hadn't hammered it in, that much I was sure of. She is a freebird now, my ribs no longer a cage for her love. No, this was a different kind of pain, a physical kind of pain, the kind of pain you only feel after falling off your bicycle or possibly being punched in the chest by your best friend. Even now I am not sure which happened. The details blur as the days grow long still the nights seem longer in a city where all inhibitions have been abandoned for the gunshots that ring out of these keys I hit like fireworks exploding out my fingertips.

& everything ends in underwear. Underwear parties after Underwear bike rides rolling mob deep on mushroom tea with me turning into an underwerewolf beneath a full moon, only two days after being arrested but a block away in a public pool, dancing naked in the swine lights at three a.m. & spending the night in jail with ten of my friends.

Then one night we set out like blue angels, boy, in beautiful formation, all hooting & hollering cause life was rich & ripe & wondrous & fast & furious & we had the hearts of men who seek new skies when Joe clipped my front tire sending me smashing into the street, spraining my wrist, but we kept rolling to the bar hitting the dance floor with blood still fresh on my arm & I screamed myself to sleep that night with my hand numb in a tub of ice. Somewhere in this mess the little lady left so I guess I can't call her that anymore.

So this is how we did all we would or could to create a summer of love in the midst of this year of death, & GodBless, but as we all know, everything is temporal. So nuzzle your noses in the Eskimo fashion for as long as possible. A dark wind she blows, times come back to go, out into the darkness of this void, Alone.

Gail Eisenhart

<u>Gail Eisenhart</u>

A native of St. Louis, Gail Eisenhart wandered from Chicago to the Gulf Coast before returning home to St. Louis in 1989. She now lives in Belleville, Illinois.

The compulsion to write grabbed Eisenhart in high school but she did not become addicted to poetry until 1995, during a creative writing course at Florissant Valley Community College. To improve her art, she attended Iowa State University's Summer Writing Festival in 1998 and Rope Walk Writers Conferences in New Harmony, Indiana, in 2000 and 2002 where she studied with poets Heather McHugh, Gary Gildner and Lynne Emanuel. Her poems have appeared in the *Saturday Evening Post, Joyful Child Magazine, St. Charles County Journal,* the *Mid-America Poetry Review* and *Mid Rivers Review.* In 2006 her review of David Wojahn's new and selected poems in his volume, *Interrogation Palace,* was published in the University of Southern Indiana *Review.*

A long-time member of the St. Louis Poetry Center, Gail served on the Board of Directors for more than five years and currently reads her poems at their Focal Point in Maplewood, Missouri. She is also a member of the metro poetry group, *Six on Saturday*, and of the St. Louis Writers Guild.

Psychotherapy No Longer Holds the Stigma It Once Did

Ah yes, I can boast about my Shrink now,
talking, talking, talking…

Sit face to face with the therapist, we'll sift facts, delve
deeper into the cause of your condition.

I blew and blew and blew until the balloon swelled
big as the lover's moon, a wondrous glowing globe.

Let's explore feelings; develop strategies to cope.
I'll help you set realistic goals; find solutions.

I tied a knot in the neck, tried to hold happiness
inside the circle of a tarnished wedding ring.

Desensitize; confront your anxiety; overcome
awkward responses. End self-destructive habits.

It didn't work; almost immediately air oozed out,
sometimes whistling, sometimes whooshing

If an unwanted situation won't change, you can;
change the way you think, behave positively.

until it emptied, became flabby, limp, lifeless—
a thing that slithered, writhing with pain

Identify troublesome thoughts. You can learn
to alleviate despair, hush anger, regain control.

into nothingness; dead on the floor, waiting for
someone to breathe life into it again.

Take tiny steps.

Exhale.

Father's Day

He enters Calvary Cemetery, follows twisted
memories in search of his father lying
peacefully (he hopes) beneath engraved granite,
feels again the pain of a life ended too soon
by suicide.

As he brushes dust from the stone,
his sons stare at the trampled grass, wonder
if they look like the man beneath the ground.
Sitting cross-legged, he tells the boys
their grandfather loves them,
would like to play catch,
          race bikes,
                    buy them ice cream…
if he could.

Fumbling in the gym bag,
he hands the boys a baseball, a pen, asks
          Would you like to leave a gift for Grandpa?
Silently, the nine-year-old takes the ball, writes
          Love, Sam
hands it to his brother
who scrawls
          +
          Jack

Ball in hand, he pats the stone,
digs into dry earth,
releases his grip.

gaye gambell – peterson

gaye gambell-peterson

Gaye Gambell-Peterson thinks of herself as an East Coast gal (born and raised in western New York), but the truth is the Midwest has claimed her. She was degreed (B.S. in Design) at the University of Michigan. Her first marriage took her to Iowa, then to California, then here to St. Louis with three children in tow. After seventeen years here, Gaye ran away to San Diego for ten years, found a better husband, brought him back to enjoy the grandchildren – now all five in the St. Louis area.

St. Louis has been good to her - although she's loved every place she's lived. In her first life here, her art career flourished. During the art fair hey-days of the 70s, her acrylic paintings and off-loom weavings put a lot of blue ribbons in her scrap box. Since the turn of the millennium, following her return to St. Louis, Gaye has successfully combined her visual art inclinations with her newer passion: poetry.

Poetry bubbled up and out in 2001, in response to one particular family relationship. Unleashed, the words kept coming. Gaye stumbled upon the St. Louis poetry community and found a home. Positive input from the St. Louis Poetry Center, Loosely Identified, Six On Saturday, and the St. Louis Writers Guild helped her to be published numerous times in literary journals. This is her second inclusion in an anthology. Gaye has a handful of second prize awards for recent poems. Her art (logos, digital collages, journal & chapbook covers) intersects the region's literary circle.

Serendipity rules Gaye's life; affirmations promise an upward spiral with a return to good health just around the corner. Two books, published in 2009, put her art and poetry together and give her more invitations to read her poetry, to revel in the spotlight. Her studio remains wonderfully messy with sticky bits for collage art, and words, words, words. She plays there; plays everywhere.

Stages of Grief

"If it was so, it might be... but as it isn't, it ain't."

~the Tweedles

Heart-startling lilt, loud
from such a small thing.
A wren, flirting with the possibility
of nesting in that rusty mailbox I keep on my deck –
the one that belonged to my father
before he removed himself with one ringing shot.
She rejects that dark place, flies away;
her song trails behind.

Raucous starling, a strutting, iridescent
bully – disagreeably selfish
when it's time to share a meal with kin
in the grass of my backyard, blowzy
with weeds and bugs.

But *it* ain't *is* yet, so there's more to consider.

A cardinal's chutzpah –
his flash and scarlet trill.
He owns the zenith
of the scraggly cottonwood tree,
the one that barely survives my ill will,
stubbornly alive in its full skirt of poison ivy.

plAine

spoken
open to judgment
just as the black bird
descends upon the
chaff after the
kernel is ground
down to bread
the reed bent
rent plucked Lucky
breeding shows
It's not the prettiness
the homily oft told
proves: homely out
yet wholeness within
The very stuff the
Vary backbone of all I
was meant to stand
for Malady shall not
sit The row of chairs
is empty
like possibilities
u n r e a l i z e d
This center so
Necessary though I
think often of eddges
those eddges where
grasse gives
way to shade-
lynds woodlynds
My salvation my
hospice here my keep
hear wHere does
(is this)
My h e a r t l y n d

Pain, Like Wind

Their spillage a scandalous exposure,
their lids roundly trespassing other yards,
garbage cans upturn all along your street.
Spewing incomplete lists, torn words, sodden tissues.
In the backyard three remaining trunks
of that ugly cottonwood lean. Only a few branches
are long enough, high enough to reach the wind,
to dance, to court a brokenness you fear.
Pain, invisible, like wind–measured by flinch or sway.
Dented trash cans, felled trees. The rattle
of well-being tumbled; the suddenness of decline.

Loy Ledbetter

Loy Ledbetter

Loy Ledbetter has lived most of his life in St. Louis, except for three years away in the Service and twelve years in employment stints around the country. His love for poetry started with reading poetry at an early age, intrigued by the sounds and rhymes. Although he wrote only sparingly as a teen, this love for poetry stayed a part of him until he began to write seriously as an adult.

Loy says, "poetry can be exhilarating, but maddening at times. Working through an opaque poem is frustrating, until finally the poem breaks free and rises. Poetry is important to the well-being of a society. Poets' eyes tend to see issues and situations from a different perspective than the mainstream media and society. This fresh vista can open a series of new thoughts and ideas. Poets are guardians of our language, protecting words and their meanings from the ambiguities thrust upon society. Their words shine with an honest accuracy." Meeting the challenge of writing, finding the exact right word is an exciting experience for him.

Ledbetter has had poems published in *MARGIE, Ozark Review,* and *The Griffin.* He has won awards in local contests. He is a past president of the St. Louis Poetry Center, serving in that capacity for many years.

Military Cemetery

They lie in geometric rows
gracing a stranger's soil.
Their bone-white crosses
bleach in the Tuscan sun.
Olives form an altar piece.
I hear them cry
in the shallow dark
for their unspent years.
From my passing window
I thank them.
I have used well
their gift of years.

Galactic Misdirection

When star upon star has blinked its last
and suns have turned to coal, our love will keep
in some black hole where we sleep
to the murmurs of centuries sliding past.

We could be the next world's Eve and Adam pair
(except for minor flaws). Though versed in apple lore
and it abundant flaws, our tastes run more
to mangos, avocados, and ruddy skin pears.

Until the next big bang, we'll sit this one out
when some super nova slings debris into space
and galactic energies set us in place.
Knowing my penchant for misdirection, no doubt

You'll spin as another Venus; I as another Mars.
In that life, too, we'll be light years apart.

Joe Wetteroth

Joe Wetteroth

Joe Wetteroth is a fourth generation St. Louis-born citizen. His family name has claimed residency primarily on the South Side since the 1880s. He is the son of two Catholic school teachers and the grandson of a Chase Park Plaza bartender.

St. Louis has created the tense setting of the bulk of Wetteroth's work. Filled with images of dirty streets and city busses, his writing is an attempt at understanding and processing his urban surroundings.

Wetteroth's primarily writes with a local group called Get Born, who performs monthly readings throughout the city. He has self-released two collaborative works. One (*Get Born #2*) with Joseph Sulier`, and another (*Sentimental St. Louis Signs of Decay*) with Mathieu Paul.

Although currently on sabbatical in Chicago, Illinois, Wetteroth is still writing about his experiences in St. Louis. He is currently working on two separate books of poetry, and plans to move back to St. Louis to continue his work.

Save Me

Save me somebody save me.
Promised myself just one night
Chasing time.
Loud Vegas Fifties bright bulbs
I see out.
I see how you could get wrapped up in
    flashing lights.

Your neighborhood is on fire,
And I'm staggering through South City,
Trying to figure out
How I'm getting downtown.

Two beers to the man on the bike.
A reasonable toll compromise
For not having any extra money,
Or a square.

In a swirling, stagnant city diners
    appear in beacons of light.
Great greasy spoon breakfast over
Yuppie conversations of confessed
    love and botched business.
Dry heaving hiccups, biscuits and gravy
    you put me on a corner
For skeleton eye taxi ride circling
    around.

Pointing out landmarks to call his
    bluff,
He tells me stories about rerouting,
Not Knowing
That there will be no more detours in
    this life.

Lincoln service, Ann Rutledge,
To and from Chicago

Four times daily.
They are dragging us through murky
water,
And I will sleep with pneumonia,
'Til I can be in your arms.

Your eyes, your kiss, warm and soft.
I try to phrase them in
Iambic Pentameter and extended verse,
But I write roses to you misspelled
and with bad punctuation.

Molly Brady

Molly Brady

Molly Brady is a lady who lives in South City, St. Louis. Her love of poetry and literature began early under the influence of her grandmother. At age ten, she purchased her first book of poetry *Falling Up* by Shel Silverstein. Brady writes with a mindfulness of the female presence as a transforming force and a love for the wonder of nature in all its complexity and truthfulness. Brady's ambitions include beekeeping, learning violin, headstands and handstands, wild animal rehabilitation, and farming. This is her first officially published work.

8 29 07

people are hanging out of open windows
screaming:

"our souls are cracked"
whispering, barely audible,
"help us."
baby children are demanding
"when will our teeth turn straight?"
is it worth such self
such self indulgence?
all masturbating to rooftop scenes
to birds with wings spread over sighing blues.
the moth is dead
while its eggs hatch in oat flour.
they are dead
with boot strings spirographing throats.

8 9 07

so you and i were born,
cut from keys.
into this neighborhood i wander,
mouth agape.
i, finding the hindquarters of a mouse
cooked on the sidewalk.
and this worm, braised by the suffering sun.
they will suffice.
oh tonight we feast.
follow me to my backyard,
the one with the garden scorched by august
and the attic fan on the 3rd floor that spins.
in my kitchen i'll cook for you
overflowing with pepper and salt.
(a pantry stocked with pepper)
oil over oil,
oil like fat,
that leaps out of cast iron
towards those shriveled brown toes and crumbling
tail.
oil that coats our skins.
smothers the wooden table,
and bowl of cucumber.
oil like water, flooding this block.

Judith Saul Stix

Judith Saul Stix

Judith Saul Stix has recently published *Woman/Years*, poems written from 1956 to 2007. This is an unusually handsome four-volume set that includes 1,234 poems, editor's and author's prefaces, a facsimile of a sequence of drafts illustrating her working methods, and an index.

Stix has written biographies, essays, reviews, and contributions to Jewish genealogy and history. Her biography *Naturalist in Mexico* has been deposited in such libraries as the American Museum of Natural History and the New York Botanical Garden. Her second biography, *Bessie Lowenhaupt from Life*, is an account in hardcover of the St. Louis painter (1881-1968).

Westgate Press has also published her chapbooks, *City of Birds* and *Sweet Length of Days, Selected Love Poems*. Her most recent publication is two essays reprinted in the anthology *Every Family Has a Story* (May 2008).

Stix was born in Atlanta, Georgia, in 1932. At Washington University she studied with Jarvis Thurston and Donald Finkel, graduating with honors in 1952. The following Spring, she married Ernest W. Stix, Jr. They have three children and six grandchildren.

The Hour

The night is cold and clear and filled
with stars. At midnight, as that real
and artificial construct called
the year is shifting numbers, you
and I, my dearest love, lie fast
within each other's arms and almost
laugh at time. Almost, almost.
If we when younger had known this free
intensity, we might have made the moon
and all these stars shine brighter still.

Untitled

Our friends are falling
like ruined cities
and we ourselves
like leaky boats
are slowly sinking,
with all the lights
still lit.

Andrea Thorsen

Andrea Thorsen

Andrea Thorsen received her M.F.A. in Poetry from Washington University in 2002, having moved to St. Louis from Michigan in 2000. Andrea received her B.A. in English and Psychology from George Mason University in Fairfax, Virginia.

Currently, Thorsen is working on her writing while spending her days as a buyer for a St. Louis book store. She believes in art. In her writing, she tries to investigate the tension between self and other, between reality and dream. One of her favorite statements on writing comes from Toni Morrison's Nobel Prize speech, "as the narrative is created, we are created by it."

Christ and the Woman Taken in Adultery
-after a painting by Max Beckmann

What if I did not ask for forgiveness,
let the mouths gap, slack like seams
undone, let them mock but did not care?
I could open my eyes to stones, only hear
you and *woman.* I could take His hand,
I could have my own intentions for it. The moon stalls
their laughter on illumination: I have not done wrong
only *I have, I am.* The blood dries
in my hair. Movement only becomes possible through
confess, reveal. For months, the glass might stay in
my knees, abdomen, until it slowly reappears
with the growth of new skin.
I imagine the shards different as they leave me, but I
know I am more easily changed.

Inscribed Plaque

I can not tell you your history,
only what may be and what is.
The way you comb your hair with
your fingers, small strokes, untying,
shows compassion, not vanity. I will give
you my body so you will never be alone,
so you will always have a language
to explain yourself.

We all know

that bleach purges the darkest movement.
We know that the roots
shrivel, white as sea foam. We are all
convinced that the knot is sharp edged
and so dissolvable. We know latex
dissolves with heat, as a dark room gives way
to windows that open to the alley, to breathing
and that breathing gives way to teeth-
intention. Because even stretched thin
there is one point of aim.

I know that over time limestone
fills the bones of a fish. That the mattock
will turn to powder what was
emptiness. I know that emptiness is easily broken.
I know that a blue pill, shattered
can wax the inside of each cavity
and that wax spills over the edge
of a bottle. The click of a lighter
repeated, that that that that
loss is winter solstice. I know skin
is a thought. Some do not believe me.

We all know that milk
does not curdle at the nipple. Because
every mouth is open. We know
a seam, closed by thread,
the color of sea foam, through and across
assumes a darkness. We know anaerobic
is a dark room where we cut
ourselves on the brass handle. We bleed closer
the needle comes, that red is circular.
We know the pit holds the fruit.

Stefene Russell

Stefene Russell

Stefene Russell grew up in Salt Lake City, in a hundred-plus-year-old house built by a notorious polygamist; it was full of spiders and secret trapdoors for hiding extra wives and children. She is the culture editor at St. Louis Magazine, former co-editor of the late 52ndcity.com and a member of Poetry Scores, a collective dedicated to translating poetry into other media. In 2007, Poetry Scores published her long poem, "Go South For Animal Index," as a beautiful little letterpress book with a full-length CD inside. She is currently working on an epic (EPIC!) work of prose-poetry that's titled, at least for now, "Orphanus."

Equinox

This is the part where I drive through Dutchtown in the springtime, trying to lose a chunk of coal in the sock of my heart.

I looked for a blue marble Pieta, and found a church called The Melvin that used to be a theater.

I was looking for an Indian mound with a diamond at its center.

I found a gleam that fell from a Cahokian's eye,
lying on the road, a lost black sequin.

I looked for a hat trick to blind me with fist fighting stars.

I found a demolition man and his pile of yellow bricks.

I looked for Our Lady of Jupiter, embroidered with purple scars,
and found a toy ballerina in a grease-trap jail.

Factory that manufactures springtime,
please glaze me senseless like your porcelain magnolias.

Give me a cherub to keep in my glove box and the choice between chlorophyll and ozone.

I can't stop driving, looking for the spot to dig
up the spring of 13 going on 14,

standing on the edge of the river,
coughing car flies out of my voice,
searching my wallet for the number
of that smart guy with pockets full of gunpowder.

The Janitor's Cello

Downtown Harp City:
clerks and secretaries drive
to cowboy bars and late-night
movie houses, oblivious

to the music of offices
and factories
after midnight.

The squeaking of garbage cans
on wheels, rumbas and talk shows
on transistor radios,

The rusty pivot of a dumpster lid,
Dripping sinks in washrooms,
the respiration of candy machines,
shredded escrow and memos
settling in trash bags,
The whine of a spray bottle
schpritizing pink chemicals
into a toilet.

The Harp Brotherhood of
Custodians is awake,
taking late buses,
unlocking closets,
spit-shining skeleton keys
and the holsters
of gum-scrapers.

Olympic Underwriting;
Helping Hand Prosthetics;
Featherweight Tool and Die;
the lights are on, and mopwater
runs black down plate-sized drains.

Excelsior Nickel-Fountain;
Red Rover Statistical Tabulation;
Goggles go on and acid baths
are applied to pernicious sink stains.

Lester Beagel cleans The Halls Bovid,
clutching a broom,
swiffing plastic grass from the base
of the lobby Christmas tree.
It's hung with hay bales
and blown glass cows. Last week
a tiny eye on the floor almost brought
his vacuum cleaner down,

and it bawled like his pawn-shop cello
at dawn when he sings out the pack
of secrets he keeps to himself in
his cinder-block house,

Songs about secrets of what these people chuck:
A jazz bit about twenty-two candy wrappers
he found drifted under a day's tabulations,
love notes on Bovid letterhead set to music,
A sad, drawly song about Bovid
logo pens still in the package

now in the trash with
prophylactics, tip sheets
and soda cans full of chaw,

Ballads of floozy secretaries,
librettos lifted form bathroom tiles,
The sad song of Sheila Rae in Dept. Q,
a whore, or so it says
on almost every floor; and also,
a ditty entitled "Milk is for babies,"
and the companion piece, "Milk grows hair on your
balls."

Right now, he knows they're dancing cha-cha
and drinking effervescent beer
Tweedy men curling moustache tips between fingers
girls scuffing their peek-a-boo heels
maybe a sweaty young clerk
will get a smile and swear to remember
that color of lipstick for all his days

Secretaries and salesmen and clerks
singing country songs into the necks
of beer bottles, oblivious to the music
of offices and factories after midnight

Lester, Lester, he thinks
if you were a knuckle-cracker,
a black cape-wearer, a guy with drain
where his heart should be, you'd tabulate
them up, you'd rat them out, you'd go on stage.
Everyone and no one
should know this much about how
the world is disinfected, how
the incinerator flue dances bluely in the dark.

Joseph Sulier

Joseph Sulier

Joseph Sulier was born and raised in the fields and creeks of Fenton, Missouri. Since then he's hung his hat in St. Louis, St. Paul, Los Angeles, Brooklyn, and Philadelphia. Sulier has been published in *Get Born* and *52nd City* Magazines. He has also appeared on KDHX's *Literature For The Halibut* and had his brain picked for *St. Louis Magazine*.

I Remembered His Face

While walking to the library
I came across a man
Old,
presumably homeless
laying sprawled on the sidewalk
half in the street
I continued walking
then turned to look again
a cane lay beside him
and he struggled to stand again
so I came to his aid
he was a heavy man
not fat
but tall
much taller than myself
took all I had just to get him halfway up
told him to grab hold of a lightpost next to him
while I could return him his cane
he apologized
"There's no need," I said
"I trust you'd do the same"
not knowing if I truly meant it
he composed himself, teetered a bit
and I continued on my way

A half hour later
as I walked back from the library
there was an ambulance in his place
and I remembered his face
in it a vision
of our modern America

It was familiar
I could remember it in the face of another
a heavy set man
whom I found face down on another sidewalk
presuming he was dead

he had been beaten severely by three young men
who passed me as I ran to help

I turned him over
discovering a disfigured face
marred beyond the recognition of what I'm sure he
actually looked like
blood had dried and covered the whole of his face
caked with blades of dead grass and gravel

A woman from the diner he was laid in front of ran
out with a towel
I propped him up
thankfully alive
and wiped away as much blood as I could
even clean it was hard to distinguish any features
both eyes swollen shut
cracked teeth
a broken nose
and a mouth that would require surgery

The grown man began to weep
right there with me
not even being able to open his eyes
to look upon me
his pain became my own
and I offered whatever words of comfort that I could
"It'll be ok, the ambulance is on its way, just sit
tight, buddy"
and we sat there waiting
his back propped up against my legs
weeping
"Oh god, oh god"

I knew exactly how he felt

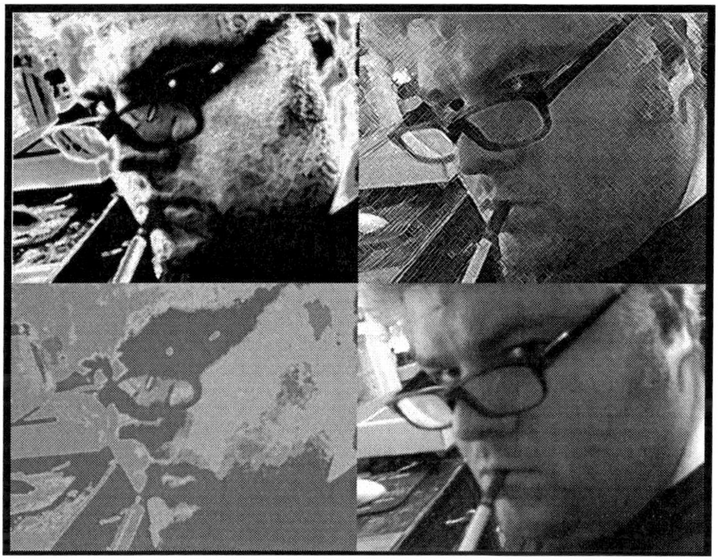

scott Thomas smith

scott Thomas smith

scott Thomas smith works in pretty much every medium. He writes poetry often, and only recently did his first painting. He's lived in St. Louis for most of his life except for a brief stint in Chicago. He wishes he could travel more. He believes in the future and in the future wellbeing of man arcs toward a nomadic lifestyle, and in the freedom to go and stay where one pleases.

When Simone De Beauvoir was asked by a normal journalistic publication what her ideas were, she said "I don't have any." She then went on to become the Simone de Beauvoir of the Existentialist Movement. Well, smith's ideas are a belief in personal immortality, free will gained by a belief in free will, and a state of eternal youth gained by solidly being oneself by, in the face of this stern re-al-is-stick wall of normalcy, that exists pre-the state-of-the-existence-of-man, in the "world" itself, ...:not having any ideas. T o live from scratch. To exist to itch. To be the thirst in the noise.

You can see all of his work currently 'published' at his website The *Neon Heart* at http://www.theneonheart.com/ including his first novel, a comic book script, a feature length screenplay, and some poetry and songs.

You're most beautiful

you're at your most beautiful
when you don't see yourself
but you better watch
what you're becoming

Chris Parr

Chris Parr

Chris Parr is a native New Zealander living in St. Louis, where he is a professor of Religious Studies at Webster University. Having been raised "downunder" in small cities by the sea, being in the Midwest is still a surprise to him.

He came to America to become involved in poetry and art, admiring the New York School, the Beats, and Robert Creely. In 1992 Chris settled in St. Louis, focusing his teaching on the religions of East Asia; he is grateful to be in a city where he can engage in performance poetry, and he has recently become involved with Get Born, thanks to the mercurial Joseph Sulier. He also has a history in rock music management.

Chris has been published over the years in a variety of magazines—*KIWI* in Auckland, *lift* and *fish* in Boston, *Black Mountain II Review* in Buffalo, *Climate* in New Zealand, *Agui* in the U.S., and *Poetry Wales*.

Chris says: "as for poetry – the outstanding NZ poet James K. Baxter once remarked that writing poetry always involves robbery; he meant that you're inevitably stealing time and attention away from what you owe your employer, your family, your friends, and myriad obligations. That remains ever true for me. That said, it's my Art, the way I can tap into the true energy-stream of what's Creative. What the poets and poems I admire share, I think, is an engagement with poetry as a form of thinking, and as an act of attention to experience as given. Humor can really help, as can Zen, as can cross-fertilization from any number of other arts. But if there's one ideal I strive for in poetry, mine and the work of any others I read, it's what someone praised in the work of one of my poet-heroes – a "'language that never forgets it is language. Get that sussed, and you've got it, made.'"

The girl on the Gatwick train to London

had a sheen of tiny golden hairs
all across the pale smooth rise and
vale of her chest in light summer shirt
when sunlight caught it at certain angles
by the opposite window. Along both slender arms
shone
a similar delicate sheen. A vista to charm with:
wheat-
fields, savanna, rushes across salt marsh, veldt.
Above,
her lips naturally pursed, full fruit
that bespoke kisses. Gleaming pale eyes, &
golden-dark hair swathed round slender neck
& shoulders. At her wrist amid bracelets
the tattered green wristband from some club or
outdoor concert. When she checked her cell-phone
for text messages, a flickering smile danced
at her lips, eyes a-sparkle with pleasure
or mischief. When she spoke to whoever called,
it was in brief spry Italian.
Tilting
her unabashed breasts with their
shimmering patina of gold into the sun's
warm glow, casually limber by the window,
a young Italian prettiest picture in the mix
all the way into London's summer
swirl

The Best Smelling Puddle in America

5 loads of laundry in &
agitating,
I'm working fast & smart on a rainy day,
coat-hangers to get from the car
& a beer while I wait –
So I grab the bottle from the car's central console,
a cold stubby of Pyramid
Apricot-flavored Ale –
reaching across the seat,
stepping back out, & in a moment's
misjudgment, catch
the bottle on some edge, &
SMASH!
it completely disintegrates, glass shards
clustered round a flat label
in a shallow puddle on
the
tarseal beneath the car,
& there it is –
(rainwater now mostly apricot-flavored
beer)
the best smelling puddle anywhere
right here
in America

Dwight Bitikofer

Dwight Bitikofer

Poet Dwight Bitikofer has worked for 32 years publishing the *Webster-Kirkwood Times* and *South County Times* newspapers in Southwest St. Louis County. Born and raised on a central Kansas farm, the world of wind and sky and horizons often show themselves in his poems. He is active among several open mic poetry groups in St. Louis. Bitikofer has twice been a featured poet at St. Louis Poetry Center's Poetry at the Point series; he has also twice performed at Poetry, Pints and Prose. He has studied with various poets at the University of Iowa Summer Writing Festival. Bitikofer has been previously published in *Untamed Ink*, *Writers' Journal*, *Mid-Rivers Review*, *Literal Chaos* and the *2009 Poetry and Prose Anthology* published by the Missouri State Poetry Society. He was among the 2009 Metro Arts in Transit Poetry In Motion winners. He was a winner in the 2009 St. Louis Writers Guild Deane Wagner Poetry Contest.

From the deck of the old house

The first evening star
millions of miles beyond
the triangle of bare walnut
branches that frame it

The horizon remembers the sunset;
the low call of an owl
wings on the breeze

From the deck of the new house

At the edge of sound
almost imagined – almost real –
a screech owl calls,
gathers dusk
in soundless trios of trills

I smile because I believe
what I thought I may have heard.

Lisa Ebert

Lisa Ebert

Lisa Ebert grew up in South St. Louis City, where the noisy rhythms of urban life remain a part of her, despite her miscellaneous homes and wanderings. After earning a Bachelor's in Communications at the University of Missouri – Columbia and making a living through disc jockeying, bartending, and slogging away at corporate communications, Lisa returned to school for an English teaching certification and later a Master's in English, both at the University of Missouri – St. Louis. She's paid her dues at the front lines of education, cutting her teeth with middle schoolers but recently settling into an Assistant Professor position at Lewis and Clark College in Godfrey, Illinois, where she is also Coordinator of the Developmental English and Reading department.

Lisa's writing takes many forms: personal essays, fiction, poetry, scriptwriting, journalism, and a graphic novel. Her work has appeared in multiple publications, including *The Riverfront Times, River Styx, Literal Chaos,* and *St. Louis Magazine*. Her original love is poetry, however, which she began writing in seventh grade, and it is the form she returns to for expressing her darkest sentiments, preferably shrouded in obscure, formalist verse. She's putting the finishing touches on her first complete volume of poetry, *Heartbreak Overload*, which explores the many break-ups life provides, romantic and otherwise. After that, should life give her a moment to catch up, she plans to dive back into fiction.

Currently residing in Kirkwood, Lisa shares her life with four energetic sons, one rock-and-roll husband, three cats, and a disparate assortment of friends: writers, artists, teachers, musicians, comedians, Stepford Wives, hoosiers, Scrabble enthusiasts, and other miscreants. They provide the inspiration, and she is eternally grateful.

On Autumn and Mars

In June of ninety-six they found a stone
From Mars with specks of dead the life long gone,
Not like the colored leaves upon the lawn,
Still steaming, breathing, like this flesh and bone.
If Mars is winter, not a comfort zone,
And Mercury new spring not quite yet dawn,
And Venus summer, gaseous to be on,
This leaves us Earth for a home all alone.
When this home is spent, the foliage gone bare,
Burnt-up carcass, life-sustaining no more,
We'll scurry for passports, tickets to soar,
And fight for the right to breathe alien air.
Will there be room for an artist who weaves
Such sentimental lines on autumnal leaves?

The Boxing Match

And the boxer, well, she cried out in her
frustration and her thwarting, *I am Leaving,*
I am Leaving, but the suitor still remains, retreating
to her corner, bell sounds, and she is dreaming,
weeping hot molten lava, her words drowning her,
I will not forget it.

The morning brings solace, for the world still turns,
and the car still runs, and "If I want to go, well, then
I shall go," but she stays, and stays, and lies on.
And the Boxer slumbers in a placid dream of
freedom, only to be awakened by a new match.

There's always more booze, more incitement, more
riot, with fisticuffs, gloves taken off, bloodied pulp of
a heart, and no trainers advising an uppercut or a left
punch, a one-two, knockout and opponent drops!
And she can't possibly know how the freedom dreams
will haunt her forever, *and forever.*

Rebecca Ellis

Rebecca Ellis

Rebecca Ellis came to the St. Louis area thirty years ago on a visit and found the best any city could offer--crumbling brick overgrown with roses, tidy bungalows, World's Fair-era grand houses, a women's professional fast-pitch softball team, the symphony, the art museum, Ted Drewes custard, Italian bakeries, and Left Bank Books. So, she did the only reasonable thing: she stayed.

She worked as a medical copy editor, a bookseller, a computer analyst, and software tester. These jobs were quite a step up, she thought, from her beginnings reading *Mad* magazine and getting part-time summer work weeding soybean fields. She wrote poems, and stopped writing, and started writing, and found other writers, and in the company of those writers she found companionable voices and inspiration.

She read poetry manuscripts for *Boulevard* magazine, served as a board member of the St. Louis Poetry Center and ran its member and high school contests for a few years, and worked with a group of women writers who eventually became known as Loosely Identified. With that group, she helped collectively edit and publish a poetry anthology of their work, and then founded Cherry Pie Press to continue publishing poetry by Midwest women writers.

Her poems can be found online at the websites of *qarrtsiluni*, *sweetlit*, and in a list of contest runners-up for a contest at *Contemporary Verse 2*. One of her poems received a free ride on the bus as part of the Metro Arts in Transit 2008 / Poetry in Motion Project. (That poem is very happy, having found the best sort of audience and a true purpose in life.) Other poems have appeared in *Sinister Wisdom*, *Hanging Loose*, *Natural Bridge*, *RHINO*, and *Quiddity*.

When recently asked about the meaning of poetry, she said, "I believe that the sound and patterns of poetry can form a bridge to allow us to move through the unknown. Poetry is a way to allow our deepest selves to experience the "other," the future, the strange, and to begin to interpret and understand. In this way, poetry both reminds us of our shared and ancient beginnings, and allows us to embrace our present and reach beyond our assumed capabilities. Imagination makes possible certain leaps, a certain faith that seems otherwise impossible."

Wisdom

I used to dream I was toothless,
I lost my hair, went to school
in pajamas. None of it
was true, but the fictions
left me breathless.
Now old, I see more clearly – I drool
on my pillow, lose car keys,
find the frozen
éclairs in the breadbox,
shapeless in a pool of melt.
I laugh at myself, and sleep
deeply and dreamless through each
long and hard-won night.

Martha Ficklen

Martha Ficklen

Martha Ficklen was born on Christmas Day, 1937, in southeastern North Carolina. She was raised by a mother and several aunts who were schoolteachers, and a saintly father. Educated in public schools in Wilmington, she went to college in Wilson, North Carolina, then moved to coastal Virginia where she married, taught school, birthed two boys now grown with families.

In 1976, Martha moved to St. Louis and continued to teach in public schools, from first grade to college. Travels include every state in the continental USA and most of the countries in Europe. Her first poetry chapbook, *The Palm Leaf Fan*, with Cherry Pie Press, is in its second printing. Martha's favorite places are libraries. Her partner for over thirty years, Nanora Sweet, is also an author.

Shadow Parade

My bedroom window faced a street
where cars passed through the night,
transforming dimly lighted walls
to screens with squares of moving light.

Some halting patterns dragged along,
merging into groups or pairs,
and others blended into streaks
that zipped around above the stairs.

Trees and houses hid the sky
and I could see no stars,
But every night around my room
I watched the passing ghosts of cars.

Julie Dill

Julie Dill

Julie Dill splits her time between her job at a West County publisher and volunteer gigs with StudioSTL, *River Styx Magazine*, Observable, and the St. Louis Poetry Center. She lives in south city with her partner Laine and their two cats, Pammy & Rudolph Yaber. Her work has appeared or is forthcoming in *Sou'wester*, *St. Louis Magazine*, *Wicked Alice*, *52nd City*, and others.

The Birds of Pontoon Beach

Harlequin Duck

Karl came back from out East in October. One month of college and he begged to come home. His dad taught math so he ran track to catch up. He jumped seven hurdles, the eighth one too high. The day after they shaved his testicles for his torn groin muscle surgery, he stitched shoulder pads into his McDonald's manager shirt. Karl's hair is soft, like a toddler's. He toughs through techno and fakes a moonwalk. He says he loves a lady who owns a Pizza Hut in Springfield. He showed me her rings strung through the chain around his neck. They were dull and bent and I said they smelled like rotten pennies and leaking batteries. So does her twat. What? Fuck you, you're not Amish.

Greater Prairie Chickens (*endangered*)

Gilly and Meyer never ran out of homophobic jokes. They made up words for scatological behavior no one ever would have thought to pursue. They laughed at themselves like it was something to strive for. Gilly's dad was the Pontoon Beach mailman, a hairier version of his short, squat son. Gilly squirted shrimper and butt pirate in mustard on buns. Meyer's car's name was Myrtle and he could turn a wet dish towel into a deadly weapon. Later a fallen airman and a heart defect died young and a shame their legacies with me are largely midnight drives to stick baloney slices on Karl B's butch black truck and the water fight that ended in six stitches and a secret.

Turkey Vultures

Tanya had the adult form of cradle cap. Her scalp was perpetually fleeing from her white-blonde hair. It escaped to her purple-shirted shoulders and huddled in clumps down her back. The dermatologist told her to stay out of dish water, but each night, she was up to her crusted, pustuled elbows in greasy, hot suds. Her husband Dale worked there, too. We called him "Grimace" behind his back, because his purple cap didn't disguise his vaguely pointed head, and his girth rolled out over the waist of his polyester pants. Together they showed me a bitter portrait of my own narcissism. Together they taught me there is love for everyone.

Great Blue Herons

Their babies would be born in parkas for the number of times they fucked in the walk-in freezer. Nathan dragged out cardboard fry boxes caved in with ass dents at least twice a week. You knew they had done it when they wore the ratty drive thru jackets and Jill-Marie blushed and Gary's braces glinted in his reflection as he smiled into the stainless steel. The stock room was warm, but it reeked of dried ketchup and besides, semen bounces when it hits the ice.

Magnificent Frigate Bird (*Accidental*)

Yvonne was old. Her frizzy gray hair sprung out from her purple visor, shading her giant plastic glasses. She smelled like pickles and pee. Every night after close, she combed the parking lot for dropped change. She used to work at the Dairy Queen with my cousin Don, ten years before. Done said one night they all taught her a lesson by sticking nickels to the concrete with construction glue. Yvonne was out there for half an hour, prying up coins with a plastic knife in the dark. Her husband only let her bathe twice a week to conserve water. Her first name was really Yolanda and for awhile, I was the only one who knew.

Double-Crested Cormorant (*Threatened*)

Charlie changed into his purple uniform in the front seat of his hatchback every day in the university parking lot. His girlfriend thought he worked at the telemarketer mall where the sports store used to be.

He kept his hat pulled down so tight he strained the seams. By day, he studied geology and accounting; evenings, he rehydrated onions and murmured citations from ethical debates and philosophical intrigues, quoted from the Wall Street Journal. Charlie called me Pinky and told me I'd be a knock out if I toned up, but sophomore year got harder so he moved to Florida.

White Pelicans

If Chicago is the city of the big shoulders, then I imagine Pontoon Beach to be the city of the ass shelf, and Granite, the city of the thigh-calf fat flap. Oh my dear fat cities, squint at me around your doughy cheeks and listen. We once hauled steel uphill both ways. We walked to work in the dark, our loaded lunch pails flashing in headlights. We let our hair air dry and we moved the toothbrush ourselves. Our hulking muscled past laughs at us, driving two blocks to the McDonalds for double quarter pounders and Diet Cokes. Release the deep-fried apple pie from your fist and sweat on.

Robert Lowes

Robert Lowes

Robert Lowes grew up in Jackson, Missouri, and as a child often imagined faraway St. Louis as resembling the Emerald City in the movie *The Wizard of Oz*. Its skyscrapers would be impossibly high and glistening, and visible from miles and miles away. When he visited for the first time in the mid-1960s at age twelve or so, he was disappointed by the skyline, which was short and grimy back then. Nevertheless, he settled down in St. Louis in the 1970s after earning a Bachelors' degree in English literature at Washington University and came to enjoy the charms of the community—its big muddy rivers, Forest Park, the Missouri Botanical Garden, the Hill, the River Road of Illinois, the historic mansions, the U. City Loop. It was a fine place to find a wife, Saundra Heisserer, and with her raise three wonderful children.

Lowes is a journalist by profession. In contrast to journalism's sanity and often formulaic prose, poetry for Lowes has been a means of converting odd, random thoughts and catchy phrases into verbal thingamajigs that might delight himself as well as an audience. He recently came across a collection of poetry by Dylan Thomas in which the author stated that he wrote his poems for the love of Man and in praise of God. That's pretty much what Lowes aspires to. His work has appeared in such journals as *The New Republic, The Christian Century, The Jabberwock Review, The Tampa Review,* and *Sentence: A Journal of Prose Poetics*. He is seeking a publisher for a manuscript titled *An Honest Hunger*. He earned a Master of Fine Arts in creative writing at the University of Missouri-St. Louis, where he received the graduate prize in poetry two years in a row. He also won the Wednesday Club Poetry Contest in 2005. Lowes is a board member and past president of the St. Louis Poetry Center, a community of poets whom he credits with helping him mature artistically, but not financially.

Tramping Through Queeny Park

I saw a crazy spray
of birds tracks in the snow,
pointed every which way,

and whether I recall
them dancing or wandering
is a minute-by-minute thing.

There were prints like broken hearts
of mule deer who escaped
the rifle cracks of fall,

a coyote's dotted line
across a frozen lake
that the snow had powdered over.

His thirst had taken him
to an open wound of water.
(I still give thanks for that.)

When I met the marks again
on a wide and civil path,
I forgave his steaming scat,

thick with rodent fur
and ribbed with a pale bone.

Good hunting, brother cur.

The Great Divide

When the earth was too tired
to spin anymore, it split into zones
of perpetual day, perpetual night.
The people of the night

left behind their drooping gardens
and caravanned toward the sunshine,
where many died on the hasty
barricades of the sun dwellers,

whose new dictator had named
the everlasting day after himself.
There, many died at their desks,
not knowing when to abandon work,

while others packed vacation bags
for the dark side to catch up
on sleep and sex in deserted mansions,
for the sun had become

an oppressive, over familiar face,
like someone who constantly stared,
repeating the same question.
A new race evolved

in the chilly nightlands,
hardy enough to subsist on starlight
and preserve some warmth at their core.
They passed a gene of contentment

to their offspring, and were spared
the ceaseless havoc of the daylands,
its blue sky criss-crossed with missiles,
its every riot at high noon.

Bad weather over there,
said the dark ones, who rejoiced
when they lifted their heads to see
a gentle rain of meteors.

Byron Kerman

Byron Kerman

Byron Kerman's favorite thing about St. Louis is the Laumeier Sculpture Park near closing time on a weekday when no one's around. It's totally boss. He writes poetry, in part, from laziness – it takes less time to work out a poem than a story (for some). But poetry is, of course, language at its most compact and powerful, so take that, psycho dwarf!

Byron has been involved in such literary endeavors as producing and performing at *Heeb Magazine* storytelling, writing comedy sketches for the Non Prophet Theatre Co., writing a monologue performed by Hydeware Theatre Co., receiving publication of some science fiction haiku (yeah, that's right) in *Star*Line* and some other poetry at *TheBeatMuseum.org*, winning the St. Louis MetroLines Poetry Contest in 1996, adding the frothy meringue of his journalistic endeavors to dozens of magazines and newspapers, bombing at various open mic nights, and reading bad poetry for five people – including his parents -- at a suburban art fair.

He plans to take it to the next level.

You Know How It Goes

you wake up, piss, let the dogs out to piss, put on your flannel robe and house shoes, get the newspaper, make some tea, feed the dogs, smoke a bowl, roll around with the dogs, put on some Coltrane, beat off to some porn with the sound turned down, order a pizza, go to take a dump, pick up the coloring book and crayons you left in there from last time, start to color but outside the lines because you don't play that shit, come out of the bathroom an hour-and-a-half later and find that you missed the pizza guy, he was there but you just must have not heard the doorbell, call them and find out they won't redeliver because you've been down that road before, make some oatmeal, give the dogs a treat, play MegaTetris on the computer, shop online for some new porn, beat off but it takes longer this time, think about leaving the house, nah—you don't feel like it, look how late it is!, take a nap, the dogs lick your face awake, let 'em out, what's on TV?, smoke another bowl, have you seen that old Clint Eastwood movie or not yet?, it's one of his Westerns, check it out, that leftover oatmeal looks good, you don't have to heat it up even cause it's good cold, call up some girl, feel like a fool, does she know you're stoned?, oh yeah—the dogs are still outside, let 'em back in, wrestle with the dogs on the floor, fall into bed, go to sleep, you know how it goes

Crucifix Balloon

You came to work on Good Friday
pulling a helium balloon
shaped like the cross
where they nailed your poor, dead savior
two thousand years ago.
It was sure cute
your crucifix balloon
like the bunnies of spring
and the jellybeans of torture
and the chocolate of blood.

I want one, too
for my little niece.
I can tie it to her stroller
and my sister can push her
through an ancient desert
hot and dry
with dream-death and sacrifice
and dung beetles crossing the dunes
singing in a trillion chirps
for me, for me
a party with balloons
all for me.

Nanora Sweet

Nanora Sweet

A St. Louisan at birth, Nan returned to the city in the 1970s to join a literary scene that still includes Left Bank Books, River Styx at Duff's, and the women's poetry group now called Loosely Identified. She is compelled by St. Louis as a European city at America's mid-continent, where Washington was never President, Hegel was a presiding genius, and Reform Judaism remains particularly strong. This city's monuments hint at empire, its bewitching lagoons and spreading brownfields at illusion, disintegration. St. Louis still has much to teach.

Educated before workshops and the M.F.A., Nan began writing to experience for herself the poetry of consequence brought to her in fine anthologies (like this one!). Her poems have won their share of St. Louis awards and gained publication here and elsewhere, including in recent chapbooks *Mix of Securities* (Snark Publishing) and *Rotogravure* (Cherry Pie Press). A participant in Loosely Identified's collection *Breathing Out*, a ten-year Board member for *River Styx* , Nan is also a teacher and scholar of Romantic writing and poetry from a woman's point of view. She gives papers, publishes essays, edits collections and sites, posts clerihews, and contributes to encyclopedias on Romantic poet Felicia Hemans and her contemporaries. Along with her membership in the English Department at University of Missouri – Saint Louis, Nan serves the University's M.F.A. Program in Creative Writing and Institute for Women's and Gender Studies.

Nan writes poetry in two styles, a Romantic ode of monumentality and myth (much of her St. Louis work in *Rotogravure*) and a classical lyric of small occasion on a plainer style (much of Nan's work in *Mix*), written with Ben Jonson as a model, or a current favorite, Rachel Hadas. *Happy Worries* is true to the plain style, which paradoxically, with its touches of Latinity, smells the most comfortably for Nan "of the lamp."

Happy Worries

Sleeplessness brings back the life I know,
an endless list of notes and still loose ends.

A scholar strays, a student disappears,
while college deans and senior colleagues frown.
I recognize them all. This is my world.

Rainfall disturbs the sky. It washes smog
away and fills the air with leaves instead.

I walk through happy worries, extra thoughts
that peaceful sleepers miss, like thoughts about

Invented Histories, an article
I've read and copied onto mismatched leaves.
We let things stray, that we may recollect.

Jay Thompson

Jay Thompson

Jay Thompson was born in Redwood City, California, in 1983 and grew up in Washington State. In college, he gave up a physics degree for poetry after reading Elizabeth Bishop and Shakespeare's sonnets.

Thompson wound up in St. Louis in pursuit of an MFA. in poetry from Washington University; he remembers jumping out of his desk chair and running around his office whooping the day he got an acceptance phone call from Carl Phillips (director of Washington University's Writing Program and one of his favorite poets). He loves this town—the red bricks, the dispersion of cultural life into individual neighborhoods (in the absence of a cool-kid district of must-see hangouts), the length of fall and spring, the Observable Reading Series, the Scottish Arms and CBGB's and Local Harvest, the unearthly late-night thunderstorms, the age, the Art Museum, Tower Grove Farmer's Market, the frozen yogurt and Bosnian food and barbecue.

He writes because of an obsession with loss, unintelligibility, double-exposures, sex, hangover breakfasts, prayer, malapropisms, and nerves. In a basic sense, it seems that poets are religious (as unmixed attention is prayer) and irreligious (as every epiphany a poet achieves is fallen away from on the way to the next poem): this contradiction demolishes and excites him.

Thompson's poems, interviews with poets, book reviews and essays have appeared here in there, in magazines like *Cranky, La Fovea, Mare Nostrum, LitRag,* and Missouri's *Pleiades* and the *Laurel Review*. He plays in two bands, co-curates the Exploding Swan reading series, co-edits a precocious and unpredictable literary journal, *Thermos* (found online at www.thermosmag.com), and is completing a manuscript of poems called *Hello*. After his M.F.A., he'll be returning to Seattle to marry an amazing woman and spend hours a day writing.

This is Jay Thompson's first experience writing about himself in the third person.

Bored

I'm bored babe / An orange tree lets a flock of
swallows settle its head / lets fruit drop / inattentively
another summer /

Someone make me a trophy / And in bored place we
have / Bored / I played Brahms for the lobsters in the
tank / I slammed my book shut so hard it / blew my
hair and mind / Seeing myself in the lobsters / or in a
clutch of quick-shedding poppies / or in a cowbone in
the grass / Things dropped / from other things rockets
shot without / quite the boost they need /

I only like this world as I frame it / through rings of
close breath on / dirty windows / sorry my last letter
was blank all / I could do was breathe on the damn
thing /

So bored I brought butterflies to the office / a plague
of yellow and iridescent blue / but they cannot class /
up existence / Consider Brahms his piano skating /
over a pond / in pursuit of a world / uncomplicated by
/ mortar and tedium then / plunged in with / barely a
glub short / a few notes the boost it needed / Always /

Surrounded by the offal of his art / even Frankenstein
sometimes / settles for TV / On the horizon wet
factories and apartments feeble sunset colors / neon
signs selling / vice he / doesn't want / A world
undeserving of his / zombies no matter / their
yawning yearning / no matter their clumsy and
examining hands

A Letter to Delmore Schwartz

Tonight, walking home, it came to me with perfect clarity:
Narcissus was wrong; the trains come whether we wait for
    them
or not, whether we're dead in the station lobby or at home
    in bed. We all worked so hard, didn't we, Delmore,
in the old days? Tonight I sat alone and watched a
    streetlight
on the corner fill with rain, scuffed the wet leaves in the
    dirt,
and thought of the carafe of wine we'd killed that night
in Koenigsplatz. Do you remember?—the dancing girl,
the sad white horse, those trees? It comes to me sometimes,
as I now imagine in must have come to you, complete
in a moment, watching two dogs, say, pursue
a third, or a bird sing in the unseasonable rain, or the
    neighbors
cut down the crowned maple in their backyard; I can take
    in
these things, but somehow all of it goes dim, subsides
back to fact. I've been thinking of you every day.—There
    was
a woman, last month, who followed me home,
drank my coffee, slept in my clothes, who stole all my
    books;
ever since then I've been drinking again, walking every
    night
(it's fall, it's the season)—quickly, and not singing,
    humming,
or even thinking of a song:
                                        I've decided it's that it's not absurd
to try to enjoy the sirens, the cheap halos the rain gives
the streetlights, the feeling of your feet sliding into your
    shoes,
so long as you don't *think*, don't resist. This, old friend,
might be where you went wrong: the mind is like an old
    light fixture
full of dead flies. (This is meant as no offense to the dust

you've since rejoined.) I can see you now—the old hotel
room,
dim and hot; you curled in bed, your fists pressed into
your face:
you opened your eyes, mistaking the phosphenes for
sunlight;
you brushed at the bed sheet, mistaking the sunlight for
dust.

Carter Revard

Carter Revard

Carter Revard has lived in St. Louis since 1961, when he began teaching in the English Department at Washington University. Born in Pawhuska, Oklahoma, he is Osage on his father's side and grew up on the Osage Reservation, where he graduated from a one-room school, serving as janitor as well as greyhound trainer, farm hand, and a usual suspect when watermelons went missing. He graduated from Bartlesville College-High, winning a radio quiz scholarship to the University of Tulsa, then a Rhodes Scholarship to Oxford, and completed the Ph.D. at Yale before teaching at Amherst College where he brought culture across the Hudson and offered watermelon to Robert Frost.

He has served on the Board of the *River Styx* Organization and helped its leaders arrange some great poetry readings at Duff's over the years. In 1997 he retired from teaching American Indian and medieval English literature, but continues to write, publish, lecture and give poetry readings in the U.S. and abroad.

Among poems published lately in the British journal *STAND* (2007-8), "Living in the Holy Land" was composed for and read at the September 2006 Lewis and Clark Commemoration under the Gateway Arch in St. Louis. In September 2008 he read poems in England and Hungary, read in April 2009 at Hartwick College, NY, in June 2009 at the Osage Cultural Center in Pawhuska; and in July 2009 lectured and read poems in Norwich, England.

His books include *Ponca War Dancers* (poems, 1980), *Cowboys and Indians, Christmas Shopping* (poems, 1992), *An Eagle Nation* (poems, 1993), *Family Matters, Tribal Affairs* (essays, 1998), *Winning The dust Bowl* (poems and memoirs, 2001), and *How the Songs Come Down* (poems, 2005). Some translations from medieval French have appeared in *The Chaucer Review* in 2004 ("The Wife of Bath's Grandmother" in heroic couplets) and 2005 ("Four Fabliaux" in tetrameter couplets--the least scabrous being "Three Dames and a Dildo"), and in 2006 in the *Revue Belge de Philologie et D'Histoire* ("A Goliard's Feast and the Metanarrative of Harley 2253").

Æsculapius Unbound
(Ovid and Darwin in Oklahoma)

By beautiful design, a snake's jawbones
unhinge, so it can swallow
things bigger around
than it is.
I wondered, when
the old man shot a blacksnake in
the hen-house, then held it
up by the tail,
just how in the hell those great big lumps
along its six-foot length, slow-twisting up and
down as it hung, had ever been
choked down.
Later, I heard that snakes
are deaf, those three hinged bones
had not yet turned into the malleus, incus
and stapes of my middle ear,
they have no tympanum
and no cochlea,
no auditory nerve, their brain only
processes earth's vibrations, but not thunder's,
so snakes don't sing, although perhaps
they dance when mating—
only their cousins, the small birds,
sing the light's changes.
So when I heard,
as twilight grew, the orchard
oriole sing its heart out there in the elm's
green heaven, something unhinged
and let the music in,
but if they hold me up and listen,
it may by then be part of me—
be how I live and breathe,
or will at least be how
I try to whistle, when
the spirit moves.

December Transients

First snow four inches deep, a half
moon white gold as twilight darkens and Blanca—
off-leash, racing in circles, panting with joy—hurls
herself
down and rolls, and snuffs, and wriggles into new
half-fluff, half-sleet gleaming beneath
dark trunks and leafless branches in
the little park, leaps up and grins
trotting back to Lawrence, who cocks his head
and looks up saying, “Geese!”
as the creaking honks come faintly down
from darkness, and overhead appear, spot-lit in
the golden lightning of the sunken sun
and soaring moon, a ragged V of geese out of darkness
floating, shifting and milling overhead,
uncertain whether to pause, and then
they reform as three move to the lead, the lines
tighten and they head southwestward into
the afterglow and are gone.
Who ever could
have thought, watching the small
dinosaurs shiver while the first
brilliant snowflakes came down into
their world so newly cold, that a small
black Border Collie would take such joy
in running through that snow
with featherless biped friends, while dinosaur cousins
with feathers, calling to the moon and sun, would soar
above them brilliant as snowflakes, on their way
into that world of living waters toward which,
this night, they fly away.

Amanda R. Wells

Amanda R Wells

Amanda Wells was born into the glory of St. Louis, raised on pork steaks and Cardinal baseball and plans to rot and die here. After a four year hiatus from this big muddy city to attend Truman State University, she returned to the familiar smell of hops and the age old question, "Where'd you go to high school?" She loves the city for its deep and underappreciated history, brick buildings on tree-lined streets and quirky corner dives. She thinks the culture's pretty unique here, too, and wants everyone in the world to know it.

For Amanda, poetry is often about writing with the smoldering ashes of the beautifully tragic. Yet she contends that the human experience is anything but bleak and hopeless. Perhaps this is due to her undying fervor for non-duality that her ancestors, the Celts, so lovingly embraced. Amanda maintains that pain can be transforming, often forcing us to recognize undiscovered strength and beauty within ourselves that wouldn't have otherwise materialized. She writes partly because she is a self-professed word slut, but mostly as a compulsion. Writing is her necessary meditation.

This meditation actualized into public writing lunacy back in January 2007 when her essay, "Seasons of Wisdom," unexpectedly won the St. Louis Writer's Guild Wired Art Essay Competition and was subsequently published in the *South County Times*. Since then, her work has appeared in *Hip Mama Magazine*, *Bad Shoe*, and in her own 'zine, *Literal Chaos*. With the madness of running Landlocked Media, she hasn't sent out as much work for publication but vows she will moving forward. She makes time for regular readings, and hosts various spoken word events across town.

Amanda plans to continue to publishing *Literal Chaos* and searching for ways to unify the local creative community. In the works also is a collection of her essays entitled *Standing Still*. She continues to write her wanderlust for the experiences of Life amid joyfully raising her daughter, Elowyn – the most divine living poem she'll ever produce.

Protesting Death by Cubicle

Melancholy is a state of familiarity
Breeding contempt among corporate pill-poppers

Who squelch their individuality
Busting the nine to five for some

White-collar criminal who sold his soul
Before the Dow took a downturn

Who pays for the concoctions that keep
Middle-class slaves chained in the status quo

As their bank-owned mud huts begin sinking
And their picket-fenced dreams start to rot.

And that's just fine for them
But not for me
Not for my conscience.

I am the woman who doesn't buy the illusion they're selling.
Stripped of my membership in the yuppie-of-the-month club,

Evicted from pseudo-privilege by stockholders
And a plane-crashed, tower-tumbled economy,

I created a life outside the lab
And understood there's more to success

Than superfluous cash to eat sushi five days a week,
Even though I hate that shit most of the year.

But keeping up appearances is the name
Of the pharmacological lifestyle game.

So have the rest of my *nori maki*, honey,

Because I’m through with it –

And you shouldn’t take Prozac on an empty stomach.

Donald Finkel

(1929-2008)

Donald Finkel

(1929-2008)

Donald Finkel's accessible, precise, frequently humorous free verse won him, among other honors, a Guggenheim Fellowship (1967), the Theodore Roethke Memorial Award (1974), the Morton Dauwen Zabel Award of the Academy and Institute of Arts and Letters (1980), a nomination for the National Book Award (1970), two nominations for the National Book Critics Circle Award, and the position of Poet in Residence at Washington University in St. Louis, where he taught from 1960 until 1991. In fourteen books of poetry and one volume of translations, his work examines the relationships between humans and animals (*What Manner of Beast*), between contemporary life and the mythological (*Simeon*), the urge to explore (*Adequate Earth, Endurance: An Antarctic Idyll/Going Under*), and, most especially, the anxieties and joys of ordinary life.

He finished his formal education at Columbia University, from which he graduated Phi Beta Kappa with a B.S. in philosophy and an M.A. in English. A brief stint as an instructor at the University of Illinois was followed by several years teaching at the University of Iowa's Writer's Workshop. It was at Iowa in 1955 that Finkel met his future wife, the poet and novelist Constance Urdang who was working toward her M.F.A. The two married in 1956 and embarked upon a yearlong Mexican honeymoon, living and writing in Mexico City and the colonial village of San Miguel de Allende.

In 1960 Finkel and Urdang settled in St. Louis, Missouri, where he joined the faculty of the English Department at Washington University. In 1977 the University instituted a graduate writing program with Urdang as coordinator, novelist Stanley Elkin teaching fiction, and Finkel running the poetry workshop.

Finkel retired from Washington University in 1991, but continued writing and publishing into the twenty-first century, until Alzheimer's disease intruded.

Constance Urdang died in 1996. Finkel is survived by his half-brother, David Finkel of New York City; daughter Liza of Portland, Oregon; daughter Amy and son Tom of St. Louis, Missouri; and two grandchildren, Annabel Rae and Jacob Elijah.

The Invention of Meaning

In the beginning was the hand
and the poem of the hand,
a breathless trope, a floating hieroglyph,
seamless as water.

The hand spoke, and the hand said,
"Let there be meaning," and the meaning sang,
"Let there be," and the hand
shaped itself another hand of clay.

Now, where there had been
but one meaning, there were two.
So the hands wrestled all night
till they saw it was pointless.

So together they shaped themselves
a cunning tongue, to arbitrate.
Now, where there had been two meanings,
there were three.

And the hands wrung one another,
abashed, and the tongue took over.

Lot's Wife

Rabid as his uncle was,
with his covenants and his
revolting rites, cringing before those
wretched Sodomites, whining,
"Take my daughters, heart-breakers,
chaste as the day they were born.
Do what you must, friends—
only spare my angels!"

There, by the gates of Zoar,
she turned away from him at last,
from that fixed grin of obeisance,
yearning over her shoulder
that wrenching homeward gaze
the Greeks call *nostalgia*,
as if home were still there,
waiting back on the plain—

The girls intact, and the man
she remembers marrying,
arms outspread for her,
framed in the ingenuous glare,
the purgative rain.

Jacob and the Stranger

Wrestled a stranger all night to a draw,
they say. Over what, they do not. Amen,
no two ways about it: this slyboots, this mama's boy,
this agile fantast wrestled a putative angel
from sundown to sun-up.

And when, at long last,
the stranger changed tack and tweaked his rival
in that occult place in the hollow of his thigh,
Jacob lost the leg-lock. Though he still had hands
(one of them cunning enough the day he was born
to keep its grip on his brother's hairy shank
as they wriggled into the light).

Yet finally,
despite Jacob's notorious lust for benediction,
despite the stranger's clever moves, the deadlock
broke at break of day. And, as the sun
lifted his molten brow to watch our hero
limp off after his wives, his women-servants,
his herds, his flocks, and his eleven presumptive
sons, escaping with his skin (though under
a pseudonym),
presumably, the inscrutable
stranger vanished, leaving Slyboots to tell the tale.